The Longest Project Ever in Human History

The Story of the Middle East

Fasil V

INDIA • SINGAPORE • MALAYSIA

ISBN 979-8-89446-712-2

Contents

Preface

Human life is an ongoing quest to comprehend the nature of reality through the subjective lens of perception. Perception, as an individual's interpretation of the world, is influenced by emotions, experiences, and cognitive distortions. Meanwhile, reality remains the actual state of things as they exist, uninfluenced by individual filters or biases.

Given the subjective nature of our perceptions, by analysing and reflecting on them critically, we can gain a deeper understanding of the world around us and align our perceptions with the true nature of reality. This critical analysis and reflection are at the core of personal growth, decision-making, and the pursuit of knowledge.

We are currently witnessing four significant geopolitical conflicts unfolding before our eyes: the Israel-Palestine conflict in the Middle East, the Russia-Ukraine conflict in Europe, instability in the Sahel region of Africa, and tensions between China and Taiwan in East Asia.

Having served in the military for a decade before transitioning into business and recently moving from Europe to the Middle East, I am deeply troubled by the ongoing conflicts and the widespread ignorance surrounding these geopolitical issues. Of particular concern to me is the enduring and intricate situation in the Middle East, a region that has been a hotbed of conflict for a century, with direct and indirect connections to the Israel-Palestine conflict. These conflicts carry the risk of spiraling into uncontrollable situations unless approached with both intellectual and spiritual maturity.

This book, "The Longest Project Ever in Human History: The Story of the Middle East," is a collection of key events related to the Israel-Palestine conflict, presented in chronological timelines, along with the thoughts and works of key stakeholders during these periods. I encourage readers to conduct further research to broaden their perceptions and perspectives, escaping the confirmation bias that might otherwise hinder competent decision-making. I hope the outcomes of the events in these timelines will not cloud our judgment but rather respect the dignity of both Israelis and Palestinians, leading to a peaceful solution that acknowledges the self-determination of both peoples.

We are all the culmination of our own perceptions, intricately woven from the tapestry of our past experiences and firmly anchored in our present reality. Our thoughts and ideologies find their roots in the diverse collections of our encounters, beliefs, and knowledge we have amassed over time. As we journey forward, where we will be is inevitably intertwined with where we came from, prompting us to embrace our past, compelling us to live consciously in the present, and actively shape our destiny for the future.

THE LONGEST PROJECT EVER IN HUMAN HISTORY

Story of the Middle East

Abraham, the Patriarch of Three Faiths (1900-2000 BCE)

Abraham stands as a central figure in the religious traditions of Judaism, Christianity, and Islam. Both biblical and Quranic accounts revere Abraham as the patriarch of these faiths, lauded for his steadfast faith in God. Believed to have resided in the ancient region of Mesopotamia (Modern day Iraq), specifically in the city of Ur, Abraham's birth is estimated to have occurred around the 19th or 20th century BCE.[1]

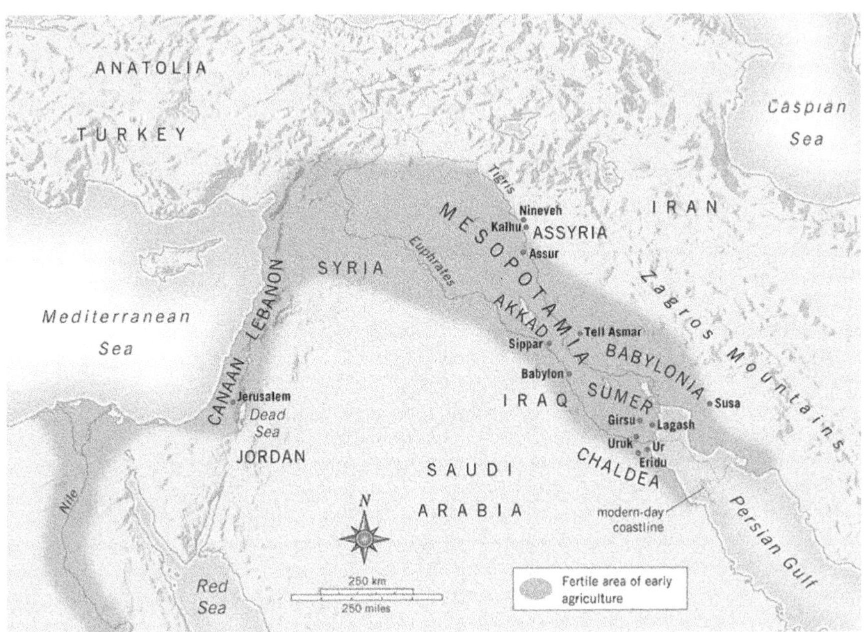

Figure 1. Fertile Crescent (Ancient Mesopotamia, 2024)

Renowned for his journey from Ur to the land of Canaan, encompassing present-day Israel, Palestine, Lebanon, and parts of Jordan and Syria, as directed by God, Abraham ultimately settled in Canaan. He fathered two sons, Ishmael and Isaac, who played significant roles in the religious narratives of Judaism, Christianity, and Islam.[2]

Ishmael is believed to have lived in the Desert of Paran, often identified with the Hijaz region in western Saudi Arabia. According to Islamic tradition, this area is associated with the valley of Bakkah, now known as Mecca, one of the holiest cities in Islam. Ishmael is considered a prophet and is regarded as the ancestor of the Arab people and the Prophet Muhammad. Ishmael assisted his father, Abraham, in constructing the Kaaba, which is considered the first house of worship dedicated to the one true God.[3]

In Biblical tradition, Isaac married Rebekah, and they had two sons, Esau and Jacob. Jacob, also known as Israel, had thirteen children with four different women, including twelve sons—Reuben, Simeon, Levi, Judah, Dan, Naphtali, Gad, Asher, Issachar, Zebulun, Joseph, and Benjamin—who became the heads of the twelve tribes of Israel. This tradition, steeped in history and faith, forms the foundation of the Israelite community and their journey through the ages.

Joseph, the favourite son of Jacob, was sold into slavery by his jealous brothers and ended up in Egypt. Despite facing various trials, he eventually rose to power, becoming the viceroy, second only to Pharaoh. His exceptional ability to interpret dreams was instrumental in saving Egypt during a famine and earned him respect and admiration.

Later, Joseph's family, including his brothers, travelled to Egypt seeking food during the great famine, unaware that Joseph was the viceroy. Joseph revealed his identity through a series of events, leading to a heartfelt reunion and the settlement of Jacob's family in Egypt.

The Israelites, descendants of Jacob, flourished in the fertile land of Goshen in Egypt. However, a new Pharaoh arose who feared their growing numbers and potential power, subjecting them to harsh enslavement and forced labour.

Moses, a member of the tribe of Levi, one of the twelve tribes of Israel, was chosen by God to lead the Israelites out of Egypt and into the Promised Land. The biblical account of this event is known as the Exodus. Guided by divine providence, they embarked on a journey through the wilderness, during which they entered into a covenant with God at Mount Sinai. This covenant, known as the Mosaic Covenant or Sinai Covenant, is a conditional agreement between God and the Israelites, who accepted specific rules of conduct in exchange for God's affirmation of them as His people.[4]

The Ten Commandments

The Ten Commandments stand as the foundation of the covenant between God and Israelites, offering a set of moral and ethical principles for righteous living. Inscribed on stone tablets by God Himself, these commandments stress exclusive devotion to God, the rejection of idols, reverence for His name, observance of the Sabbath, and honouring one's parents. They also strictly forbid murder, adultery, theft, bearing false witness, and coveting.[5]

The Divine Promise

Shortly before entering the Promised Land of Canaan, the Deuteronomic Code is revealed in the Book of Deuteronomy. Presented as a farewell address by Moses to the Israelites, this code includes laws crucial for the well-being of the people in the land they are about to possess.[6]

1. *And it will be, when all these things come upon you the blessing and the curse which I have set before you that you will consider in your heart, among all the nations where the Lord your God has banished you.*

2. *and you will return to the Lord, your God, with all your heart and with all your soul, and you will listen to His voice according to all that I am commanding you this day you and your children,*

3. *then, the Lord, your God, will bring back your exiles, and He will have mercy upon you. He will once again gather you from all the nations, where the Lord, your God, had dispersed you.*

4. *Even if your exiles are at the end of the heavens, the Lord, your God, will gather you from there, and He will take you from there.*

5. And the Lord, your God, will bring you to the land which your forefathers possessed, and you [too] will take possession of it, and He will do good to you, and He will make you more numerous than your forefathers.

(Deuteronomy 30:1-5)

This prophecy has been interpreted in various ways, including its application to the Babylonian exile and the eventual return of the Jewish people to their homeland.

Entry into the Promised Land and the Era of Judges

After their challenging journey through the wilderness, Joshua, Moses' appointed successor, led the Israelites across the Jordan River into the long-awaited Promised Land of Canaan. Aaron, Moses' brother, assumed the role of the first High Priest.[7]

Subsequently, in the 10th century BCE, King David established the kingdom, which was later strengthened by his son, King Solomon. Around 960 BCE, Solomon constructed the First Temple on Mount Moriah, also known as the Temple Mount, in Jerusalem. This site holds great significance in biblical tradition as the location where Abraham was instructed by God to sacrifice his son Isaac as a test of faith. According to the Book of Genesis, an angel intervened at the last moment, sparing Isaac's life and providing a ram for the sacrifice instead.[8]

The temple was a central place of worship and assembly for the Jewish people, housing the Ark of the Covenant and serving as a symbol of their faith and national identity. During this pivotal period, the Israelites settled in the territory, forming a confederation of tribes that eventually culminated in the kingdom of Israel. This era, marked by the governance of judges, witnessed recurring cycles of obedience, apostasy, and divine intervention.[9]

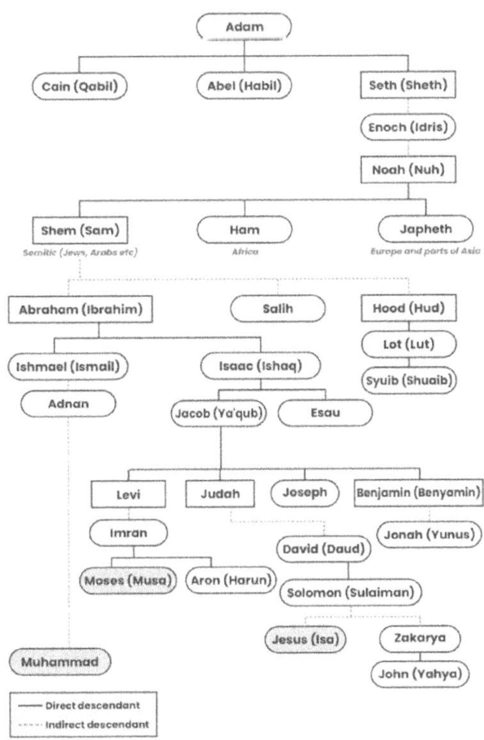

Figure 2. Genealogical tree (Arabes du nord, 2018)

The destruction of the First Temple

Following the reign of King Solomon, Israel split into two kingdoms: the northern kingdom of Israel and the southern kingdom of Judah. The northern kingdom fell to the Assyrians in 722 BCE, leading to the exile of its inhabitants, who became known as the Ten Lost Tribes of Israel. The southern kingdom of Judah later succumbed to the Babylonians in 586 BCE, resulting in the destruction of the First Temple (Solomon's Temple) and initiating the Babylonian Exile.[10]

Beginning of Jewish Diaspora

Many of Judah's inhabitants were forcibly exiled to Babylon, enduring several decades of captivity and displacement. A significant turning point occurred with the rise of Cyrus the Great, the Persian king who conquered the Babylonian Empire in 539 BCE. Cyrus's decree allowed exiled peoples, including the Jews, to return to their homelands and rebuild their temples, marking the end of the Babylonian Exile and the beginning of the Persian period.[11]

The period following the return from exile was marked by significant geopolitical shifts and cultural exchanges under various empires, including the Persian, Greek, and Roman empires. Throughout these tumultuous times, prophets emerged as voices of spiritual guidance and encouragement, urging the people to maintain their faith and commitment to their covenant with God.

During the 1st century BCE to the 6th century CE, Jews settled in various regions of the Roman Empire, including Rome and Alexandria, where they established vibrant communities. However, in 19 CE, Emperor Tiberius ordered the expulsion of Jews from Rome, marking one of the early instances of persecution due to their alleged involvement in protests, participation in Egyptian cults, and rumours of mass conversions to Judaism.[12]

Destruction of the Second Temple: A Turning Point in Jewish History (70 CE)

The First Jewish-Roman War, also known as the Great Jewish Revolt, was a major conflict between the Roman Empire and the Jews of Judaea that lasted from 66 to 73 CE. The war culminated in a devastating siege of Jerusalem by Roman legions under the command of the future emperor Titus in 70 CE. The Temple, a symbol of Jewish identity and worship, was razed, along with much of Jerusalem.[13] The aftermath saw a significant loss of life among the city's inhabitants, with many being killed or enslaved. This tragic event is remembered annually by Jews on the fast day of Tisha B'Av.[14]

The destruction of the Second Temple led to a major shift in Judaism. With the Temple gone, the sacrificial system mandated by the Torah ceased, prompting a fundamental change in religious practices. Rabbinic Judaism emerged as the dominant form of worship, focusing on synagogues and Torah study. Politically, the Temple's destruction signified the loss of Jewish sovereignty in Israel, prompting migrations that shaped Judaism and Jewish identity for centuries.[15]

Christianity and Byzantine Empire

In the period just before the destruction of the Second Temple in 70 CE, two significant figures resided in the region: Jesus of Nazareth and John the Baptist. Jesus, believed to have been born between 6 BCE and 4 BCE, hailed from the Tribe of Judah, one of the twelve tribes of Israel, and was a descendant of King David and Solomon. In the Arab world, Jesus is known as Isa ibn Maryam, while John the Baptist is known as Prophet Yahya.[16]

At the age of 30, Jesus underwent baptism—a religious ritual symbolizing purification or initiation into the faith—administered by John the Baptist, a Jewish preacher active in the area of the Jordan River in the early 1st century CE. This baptism marked the beginning of Jesus' mission to fulfil the law.[17]

Jesus preached about the Kingdom of God, prioritizing love, forgiveness, compassion, and salvation over strict adherence to religious laws. Through parables, he challenged the religious norms of the time, posing a threat to the power and status of the Jewish authorities.[18] According to the gospel accounts, Jewish authorities in Roman Judea accused Jesus of blasphemy and sedition. They brought him before Pontius Pilate, the Roman governor of the province, who ultimately approved Jesus' crucifixion[19]

This event is described in the Bible, in Matthew 27:22–25.[20]

22 "What shall I do, then, with Jesus who is called the Messiah?" Pilate asked.

They all answered, "Crucify him!"

23 "Why? What crime has he committed?" asked Pilate.

But they shouted all the louder, "Crucify him!"

24 When Pilate saw that he was getting nowhere, but that instead an uproar was starting, he took water and washed his hands in front of the crowd. "I am innocent of this man's blood," he said. "It is your responsibility!"

25 All the people answered, "His blood is on us and on our children!"

This event led to the belief that the Jewish people collectively bear responsibility for the crucifixion of Jesus Christ, known as the concept of Jewish deicide. This notion has been deeply contentious throughout history, shaping theological discourse and fuelling anti-Semitic sentiments. It has incited violence against Jewish communities, led to expulsions from various countries, and facilitated torture in subsequent years.[21]

Following Jesus' crucifixion, his disciples spread the Gospel throughout the Roman Empire and beyond. The early Christian community grew rapidly, attracting both Jews and Gentiles and establishing churches in various cities. A significant turning point in Christian history was the conversion of Roman Emperor Constantine the Great in the 4th century CE. In 330 CE, Constantine established Constantinople (modern-day Istanbul) as the new capital of the Roman Empire, shifting the centre of power from Rome to the eastern Mediterranean region.[22] After Constantine, the eastern Roman Empire, ruled from Constantinople, became known as the Byzantine Empire. By the reign of Emperor Justinian (527–565 CE), it had fully emerged as a distinct entity characterized by the use of Greek language, Hellenistic culture, and a profound emphasis on Christianity. Justinian's rule is renowned for its ambitious projects, military campaigns, and the codification of Roman law, representing the zenith of Byzantine power and influence.[23]

Fall of the Western Roman Empire (476)

The fall of the Western Roman Empire, commonly referred to as the fall of Rome in 476 CE, marked the end of centralized Roman authority in the western provinces. This event, signified by the deposition of the last Western Roman Emperor, Romulus Augustulus, by the Germanic chieftain Odoacer, was the culmination of various factors. These included barbarian invasions, internal conflicts, economic downturns, administrative difficulties, and military vulnerabilities. Consequently, political power fragmented in Western Europe, paving the way for the emergence of new political entities and the transition to the medieval period.[24]

This marked the shift from classical antiquity to the Middle Ages, often termed the "Dark Ages." This term is often used interchangeably to describe the period in European history spanning from the fall of the Western Roman Empire to the onset of the Renaissance, approximately from the 5th to the 15th centuries.[25]

Islam and rise of Khalifate

Prophet Muhammad, believed to be a descendant of Ishmael, the son of Abraham, was born around 570 CE in Mecca, Arabia. His early life was marked by hardships, including the loss of both parents. Tradition holds that Muhammad received revelations starting at the age of 40, documented in the Quran, Islam's holy scripture. These teachings emphasize monotheism and provide guidance for moral conduct and societal justice.[26] Following Prophet's death in 632 CE, the caliphate emerged as a central institution in early Islamic history. The Rashidun Caliphate, known as the "Rightly Guided Caliphate," was led by four successive caliphs who were companions of Prophet Muhammad: Abu Bakr, Umar ibn al-Khattab, Uthman ibn Affan, and Ali ibn Abi Talib (632-661 CE).[27]

The Rashidun Caliphs are renowned for their administrative advancements and military conquests, which laid the groundwork for subsequent Islamic Caliphates. Caliph Umar ibn al-Khattab, aided by the renowned military commander Khalid ibn al-Walid, led the conquest of the Levant region from the Byzantine Emperor. Following a four-month siege, Jerusalem surrendered peacefully in 637 CE, with Umar personally overseeing negotiations and signing a treaty with the Christian Patriarch Sophronius. This agreement guaranteed the safeguarding of the city's sacred sites and extended religious freedom to Christians.[28]

Upon entering the city, Umar went to the Foundation Stone at Temple Mount, known to Muslims as Haram el Sharif (the Sacred Noble Sanctuary), believed to be the site from which Prophet Muhammad had a mystical night journey known as the Me'raj.[29]

The Foundation Stone is revered as the holiest site in Judaism, believed to be where God created the world, formed the first human, Adam, and witnessed significant events like the Binding of Isaac and the presence of the Ark of the Covenant in the First Temple.[30] Adjacent to the Foundation Stone to the south lies Masjid al-Aqsa, regarded as the third holiest site in Islam after the Masjid al-Haram in Mecca and the Prophet's Mosque in Medina. It was towards this direction, the Bayt al-Maqdis or the Temple Mount that Muslims initially prayed before the Qibla (direction that Muslims face during their prayers) shifted to the Kaaba in Mecca in 624 CE by Prophet Mohammed.[31]

Umayyad Caliphate (661–750)

A few decades later, following the First Muslim Civil War also known as First Fitna, the Umayyad Caliphate (661–750 CE) emerged.[32] Muawiyah-I assumed the caliphate after the assassination of Caliph Ali, Prophet Muhammad's son-in-law and the fourth caliph of the Rashidun Caliphate, in 661 CE. The Umayyads shifted the capital from Medina to Damascus and extended their dominion across North Africa, Spain, and Central Asia.[33]

During this period, the Dome of the Rock was erected over the Foundation Stone between 685 and 691 CE under the patronage of Caliph Abd al-Malik. The Dome of the Rock features a magnificent golden dome adorned with elaborate mosaic designs, complemented by its octagonal form, showcasing a harmonious blend of Byzantine, Persian, and early Islamic architectural influences.[34]

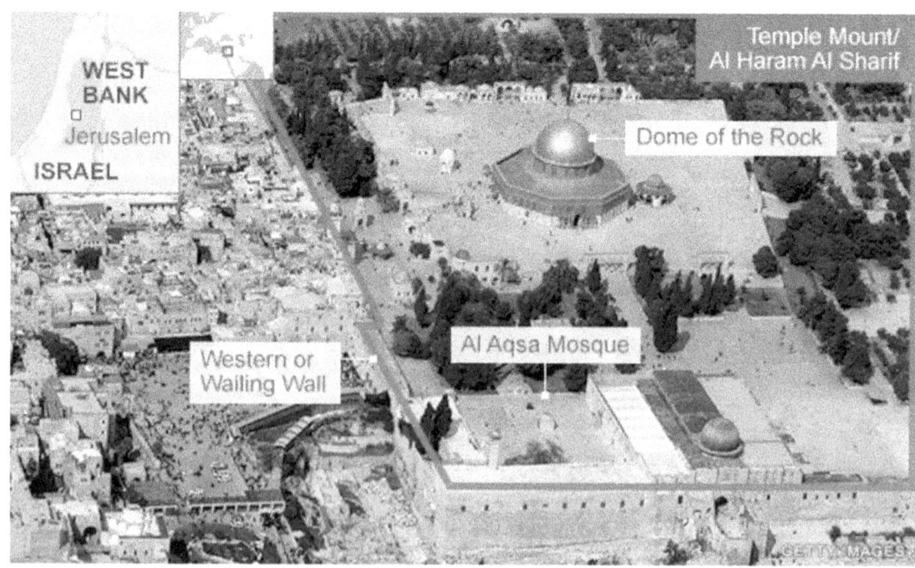

Figure 3. Temple Mount (BBC,2021)

The Golden Age of Islam and Sephardic Jewry

Following the Umayyads, the Abbasid Caliphate (750–1258) rose to prominence, establishing Baghdad as its capital. This era marked the Golden Age of Islam, during which Muslim scholars significantly advanced science, philosophy, mathematics, astronomy, medicine, and literature by preserving and translating works from ancient civilizations such as Greek, Roman, Persian, and Indian into Arabic.[35] This translation movement played a crucial role in transmitting classical knowledge and laying the groundwork for future intellectual progress.[36]

The spread of written knowledge was greatly facilitated by innovations in printing technology, likely acquired from Chinese prisoners of war following the Battle of Talas against the Tang Dynasty in 751 AD. Unlike in China, where papermaking was primarily reserved for the elite, the Arabs quickly adapted and expanded production, establishing paper mills that made books more accessible to a broader audience.[37]

The House of Wisdom, also known as Bayt al-Hikmah, was a renowned public academy and library in Baghdad during the Abbasid era. Established on either by Harun al-Rashid or al-Mansur, it became a centre for scholarly activities and translations.[38]

	Contributor	Time Period	Contributions
1	Al-Khwarizmi	c. 780–850	Father of Algebra; introduced Hindu-Arabic numeral system. He published Al-Kitāb al-Mukhtaṣar fī Hisāb al-Jabr w' al-Muqābala (The Compendium Book on Calculating by Rejoining and Balancing), from which the term 'algebra' (al-jabr) was derived.

	Contributor	Time Period	Contributions
2	Al-Kindi	c. 801–873	Known as "Philosopher of the Arabs"; contributions to philosophy, mathematics, astronomy, and medicine, Crucial role in translating Greek philosophical works into Arabic
3	Al-Zahrawi (Abulcasis)	936–1013	Surgeon and physician; Known as the "father of modern surgery" and introduced over 200 surgical instruments, wrote "Al-Tasrif," a thirty-volume medical encyclopedia
5	Ibn Sina (Avicenna)	980–1037	Polymath; author of Kitab Al-Qanun Fil-Tibb, also known as "The Canon of Medicine", Written over 450 works. The Qanun (Canon) was translated in Latin in the 12th century and used as a predominant medical text for around 6 centuries.
6	Ibn al-Haytham (Alhazen)	965–1040	Pioneer of the scientific method and experimental physics; Groundbreaking work on optics, His most famous work, "Kitab al-Manazir" (The Book of Optics), presented a new theory of vision based on empirical observations and experimentation.
7	Al-Biruni	973–1048	Contributions to astronomy, mathematics, geography, and anthropology, Notable work 'Taḥqīq mā li-l-hind,' earned him the title 'founder of Indology'. "The Chronology of Ancient Nations," provides a universal anthropological account
8	Omar Khayyam	1048–1131	Mathematician, astronomer, and poet; author of the "Rubaiyat" a collection of quatrains reflecting on life, love, and philosophy

	Contributor	Time Period	Contributions
9	Al-Ghazali (Algazelus)	1058–1111	Theologian, philosopher, and jurist; influential works on Islamic spirituality and philosophy. notable works include "The Revival of the Religious Sciences" (Iḥyā' . 'Ulūm al-Dīn), "The Incoherence of the Philosophers" (Tahāfut al-Falāsifah), and "The Alchemy of Happiness" (Kimiya-yi Sa'ādat).
10	Averroes (Ibn Rushd)	1126–1198	Philosopher and jurist; contributions to Aristotelian philosophy and Islamic jurisprudence; Work "The Incoherence of the Incoherence" (Tahāfut al-Tahāfut), defended the compatibility of reason and religion, His commentaries on Aristotle's works played a key role in the development of Western philosophy during the Middle Ages.
11	Ibn al-Nafis	1213–1288	Physician; contributions to anatomy and cardiovascular physiology, notable work is "Sharh Tashrih al-Qanun" (Commentary on the Anatomy of Canon), where he described the pulmonary circulation of blood
12	Ibn Battuta	1304–1368/69	Scholar and traveller; extensive travels documented in "Rihla"
13	Ibn Khaldun	1332–1406	Historian, sociologist, and philosopher; authored "The Muqaddimah"
14	Al-Ma'arri	973–1057	A poet, philosopher, and sceptic known for his literary works and philosophical writings
15	Al-Jazari	1136–1206	An engineer and polymath who made significant contributions to mechanical engineering, renowned work, "The Book of Knowledge of Ingenious Mechanical Devices,", referred to as the "father of robotics"

	Contributor	Time Period	Contributions
16	Nasir al-Din al-Tusi	1201–1274	A polymath known for his contributions to mathematics, astronomy, philosophy, and theology
17	Ibn al-Shatir	1304–1375	An astronomer and mathematician who made important advancements in understanding planetary motion

Table 1. Golden Age scholars (Al-Djazairi, S.E. 2018)

" The seeker after truth is not one who studies the writings of the ancients and, following his natural disposition, puts his trust in them, but rather the one who suspects his faith in them and questions what he gathers from them, the one who submits to argument and demonstration and not the sayings of human beings whose nature is fraught with all kinds of imperfection and deficiency. Thus, the duty of the man who investigates the writings of scientists, if learning the truth is his goal, is to make himself an enemy of all that he reads, and, applying his mind to the core and margins of its content, attack it from every side. he should also suspect himself as he performs his critical examination of it, so that he may avoid falling into either prejudice or leniency."

– Ibn al-Haytham

During this medieval period, Sephardic Jewry flourished in the Iberian Peninsula under the Abbasid Caliphate, known as the Golden Age of Jewish culture. Sephardic Jews made significant contributions in fields such as philosophy, science, medicine, literature, and linguistics. This era fostered a vibrant exchange of ideas and culture among Jews, Muslims, and Christians, enriching the cultural and intellectual landscape of the region.[39]

Contributor	Period	Explanation
Moses ben Enoch	(c. 853-940)	Leading figure in Hebrew grammar and linguistics; standardized Hebrew language, paving the way for future scholarship and literature.
Hasdai ibn Shaprut	(c. 915-970)	Diplomat and patron of scholars; fostered cultural exchange, translated Greek and Latin works into Arabic, and protected Jewish communities.
Menahem ben Saruq	(c. 920-970)	A Jewish lexicographer and poet who composed the first Hebrew-language dictionary, a lexicon of the Bible. His work was significant in the development of Hebrew literature and language.
Solomon ibn Gabirol	(c. 1021-1058)	Philosopher and poet blending Jewish theology with Neoplatonic and Aristotelian philosophy; influential in both Jewish and Islamic thought.
Maimonides (Rambam)	(c. 1135-1204)	A renowned medieval Sephardic Jewish philosopher, physician, and Torah scholar. His works had a profound impact on Jewish philosophy, law, and ethics. He also wrote extensively on medicine.

Table 2. Golden Age Jewish Scholars (Encyclopaedia Britannica, 2024)

Massacre of Granada (1066)

The Massacre of Granada is a tragic event that occurred on December 30, 1066, in Granada, Spain, during Muslim rule in al-Andalus. This massacre involved a Muslim mob storming the royal palace, crucifying the Jewish vizier Joseph ibn Naghrela, and approximately 1000 Jewish residents were killed, marked the end of the Golden Age of Spanish Jewry. The massacre's causes are multifaceted, stemming from religious, political, and social tensions. It unfolded during a period of regional political turmoil, exacerbated by the Crusades and shifting alliances among Muslim factions. Many Jews fled Granada afterward, while some returned, but life for them never regained its former stability.[40]

Judah Halevi (1075-1141)

Judah Halevi, a renowned philosopher and poet of the Golden Age, eloquently expressed a profound yearning for Zion in his writings. The term 'Zion' originates from the Hebrew Bible, symbolizing the Land of Israel and Jerusalem. In his renowned work, 'Sefer ha-Kuzari,' Halevi presented a comprehensive philosophy of the Land of Israel, emphasizing its unique status as the Holy Land. His poetic verses, notably the iconic line, 'My heart is in the East, and I am at the end of the West,' encapsulated the essence of Jewish longing for Jerusalem and the Land of Israel. Halevi's passionate calls for a return to Zion resonated deeply with Jews throughout the diaspora and laid the groundwork for future Zionist aspirations.[41]

Jerusalem's Shifting Powers (1099-1250)

Amidst these developments, Jerusalem experienced significant power shifts. In 1099 CE, Christian Crusaders from the First Crusade captured the city from the Fatimid Caliphate, restoring it to Christian rule and establishing the Latin Kingdom, which included the revered Church of the Holy Sepulchre. Following the conquest, French nobleman Godfrey of Bouillon was elected to govern the new Christian state as the King of Jerusalem.[42]

However, in 1187 CE, Sultan Saladin, the founder of the Ayyubid dynasty (1171 - 1260 CE), reclaimed Jerusalem. Under his leadership, the city embraced religious tolerance, with agreements facilitating Christian pilgrimage access.[43] Subsequently, in 1250 CE, Jerusalem came under the rule of the Mamluk Sultanate, a military class of slave soldiers who later rose to power and established their own ruling dynasty. They governed Jerusalem and other regions until the city was conquered by the Ottomans.[44]

The Expulsion of Jews from England (1290)

In 1290, King Edward I of England ordered the expulsion of all Jews from the country by November 1, under the threat of execution. Around 2,000 Jews were exiled, with only a few opting to convert to Christianity.[45] The Tower of London became the main departure point for Jews leaving England, with a deportation tax imposed on them. This expulsion had a lasting impact by embedding antisemitism into English culture, and the edict remained in force for the rest of the Middle Ages until it was overturned during the Protectorate in 1656, allowing Jews to resettle in England. The antisemitic sentiment in England led to violent outbreaks, such as the massacre of Jews in York in 1190, and the imposition of discriminatory laws.[46]

Alhambra Decree (1492)

The Reconquista, spanning from the 8th to the 15th century, marked a prolonged effort by Christian kingdoms to reclaim the Iberian Peninsula from the Muslim rule of the Abbasid and Umayyad Caliphate. This protracted struggle culminated in pivotal events such as the Battle of Covadonga and the fall of Granada in 1492. Subsequent to the Reconquista, Spain instituted religious homogenization policies, notably the expulsion of Jews and Muslims.[47]

The Alhambra Decree of 1492, issued by the Catholic Monarchs of Spain, mandated the expulsion of practicing Jews from the Crowns of Castile and Aragon, alongside their territories and possessions, by July 31 of the same year. The persecution preceding this decree, coupled with its enforcement, prompted over 200,000 Jews to convert to Catholicism, while between 40,000 and 100,000 were forcibly expelled. This decree precipitated the dispersal of Sephardic Jews across Ottoman lands and Europe, and they have survived to this day in countries such as Egypt, Algeria, Morocco, Turkey, Greece, and Bulgaria.[48]

Meanwhile, Ashkenazi Jews migrated eastward, settling in Eastern Europe, particularly in Poland-Lithuania and the Russian Empire. Despite periodic pogroms, they established thriving communities characterized by the development of the Yiddish language and culture, contributing significantly to commerce and scholarship.[49]

Golden Age to Renaissance

The decline of the Golden Age of Islam coincided with various socio-political factors, including the Mongol invasions (13th to 14th centuries), internal conflicts, and the rise of competing powers. However, its legacy continued to influence the Renaissance in the West (14th to 17th centuries). The rediscovery of ancient texts, made possible by translation efforts and the exchange of knowledge and ideas from the Islamic world during the Middle Ages, played a pivotal role in shaping the intellectual landscape of the Renaissance.[50]

Characterized by a revival of classical antiquity, humanism, and the exploration of individual potential, which fuelled remarkable progress in art, literature, science, and philosophy. Renowned figures like Leonardo da Vinci, Michelangelo, Raphael, Niccolò Machiavelli, Thomas More, Galileo Galilei, and Johannes Kepler emerged during this period. Johannes Gutenberg's invention of the printing press transformed communication, while humanist scholars emphasised education, paving the way for the Enlightenment.[51]

The Ottoman Conquest of Jerusalem

The Ottomans conquered Jerusalem, in 1517 during the reign of Sultan Selim I. This conquest was part of Selim's broader campaign against the Mamluk Sultanate, which controlled Egypt, the Levant, and the Hejaz.[52] The victory at the Battle of Marj Dabiq near Aleppo allowed the Ottomans to annex these territories, significantly expanding their empire. The Ottomans undertook several important architectural and civic projects in the city, including the restoration of the Dome of the Rock and the Al-Aqsa Mosque. The Walls of Jerusalem built by Sultan Suleiman the Magnificent, are one of the most prominent remnants of Ottoman architecture in Jerusalem today. The Ottomans allowed the reconstruction of religious sites like the Church of the Holy Sepulcher and promoted coexistence among different religious communities.[53]

The Ottomans began as a small Turkic principality in Anatolia (modern-day Turkey). They rapidly expanded their territory through military conquests, strategic marriages, and alliances. The capture of Constantinople in 1453 by Sultan Mehmed II, also known as Mehmed the Conqueror, marked a significant turning point, as it established the Ottomans as a dominant power in the Eastern Mediterranean and brought an end to the Byzantine Empire.[54] The decline of the Ottoman Empire began in the late 17th century due to military defeats, internal strife, and rising European powers.[55]

The Evolution of Zionism: From Longing to Action

Zionism, a nationalist movement originating in the 19th century, aimed to create a homeland for the Jewish people in Palestine, aligning with the Land of Israel in Jewish tradition. There are notable personalities and their works who proposed the idea even before the 19th century.

Moses Hess (1812-1875)

Moses Hess, a German Jewish philosopher and socialist, advocated for Jewish nationalism and self-determination. Influenced by secular and socialist ideas, he argued for the establishment of a Jewish state in Palestine to address the challenges faced by Jews in Europe, known as the "Jewish question." His influential work, "Rome and Jerusalem: The Last National Question," laid the groundwork for the Zionist movement and inspired leaders like Theodor Herzl.[56] Despite initial scepticism, Hess's ideas gained traction, contributing to the emergence of Zionism as a significant political force in the late 19th century.

Leon Pinsker (1821-1891)

Growing up in the Russian Empire, Leon Pinsker witnessed the rampant anti-Semitism that plagued Jewish communities firsthand. These experiences ignited his fervent advocacy for Jewish rights and self-defence, ultimately leading to the publication of his influential pamphlet, "Auto-Emancipation." In this seminal work, Pinsker argued that true emancipation and security for Jews could only be achieved through the establishment of their own independent state. "Auto-Emancipation" served as a catalyst for the Zionist movement, laying down the ideological groundwork for the pursuit of a Jewish homeland in Palestine.[57] Pinsker's impassioned advocacy resonated deeply with Jews worldwide, significantly advancing the Zionist cause.

Eliezer Ben-Yehuda (1858-1922)

Eliezer Ben-Yehuda, a pioneering figure in the revival of Hebrew, played a crucial role in shaping modern Israel's cultural and linguistic identity. He believed that Hebrew was vital for the national reawakening of the Jewish people and dedicated himself to promoting its use as a spoken language. Through his relentless efforts, which included the establishment of Hebrew newspapers and dictionaries.[58] Additionally, he was actively involved in the early Zionist movement, advocating for Jewish immigration to Palestine.

The First Aliyay (1881-1903)

The First Aliyah, also known as the agricultural Aliyah, was a significant wave of Jewish immigration to Ottoman ruled Palestine between 1881 and 1903. Following widespread pogroms in the Russian Empire, notably the "Kiev Pogrom" of 1881, Leon Pinsker's pamphlet "Auto-Emancipation!" and the establishment of the organization "Hibbat Zion" (a collection of proto-Zionist organizations) catalysed a national awakening among Jews in the Pale of Settlement (western region of the Russian Empire) and beyond.[59]

The pivotal Focşani Zionist Congress of 1882, attended by thousands, outlined plans for organized immigration and the establishment of farming communities known as Moshava. The Jewish population in Ottoman Palestine increased from around 26,000 to approximately 55,000 by the end of the First Aliyah.[60]

Christian Zionism (1884)

Christian Zionism originated in the 19th century, primarily in the UK and US. Christian Zionism is a multifaceted political and religious ideology advocating for the return of the Jewish people to the Holy Land, seen as fulfilling biblical prophecies and a prerequisite for the Second Coming of Jesus Christ.[61]

Dispensationalist Christianity, a key framework, sees Israel's establishment as pivotal for Jesus' return. While some Jewish discomfort persists, William Hechler (1845–1931) British Anglican priest and theologian played a significant role in the Christian Zionist movement. He organized a committee of Christian Zionists to aid Russian Jewish refugees relocating to Palestine following pogroms, which were violent riots aimed at massacring or expelling an ethnic or religious group. In 1884, Hechler authored a pamphlet titled "The Restoration of Jews to Palestine According to the Prophets." He later developed a close relationship with Theodor Herzl, advocating for Herzl's ideas outlined in his book "The Jewish State." Hechler also facilitated a meeting between Herzl and Kaiser Wilhelm II to discuss the establishment of a Jewish state. Their friendship persisted until Herzl's death in 1904.[62]

Theodor Herzl: The Father of Political Zionism

Theodor Herzl, also known as Binyamin Ze'ev Herzl, was a key figure in history as the visionary architect of political Zionism and the driving force behind the creation of the modern State of Israel. Born in 1860 in Austro-Hungary, he envisioned a Jewish homeland free from persecution, earning him the title "Hozeh HaMedinah" or the Visionary of the State. Herzl's influential book "Der Judenstaat" (The Jewish State) and his efforts led to the First Zionist Congress in 1897, laying the groundwork for the Zionist movement.[63]

Herzl's evolution into the foremost figure of Zionism was catalysed by the widespread anti-Semitism that permeated Europe during his lifetime, notably exemplified by the Dreyfus Affair in France.[64] The Dreyfus Affair, a notorious political scandal in France, had far-reaching implications for French society, politics, and Jewish identity. In 1894, Captain Alfred Dreyfus was falsely accused of espionage for passing military secrets to the German Embassy in Paris. Despite weak evidence and entrenched anti-Semitic prejudices, Dreyfus was wrongfully convicted and sentenced to life imprisonment on Devil's Island. Doubts persisted, leading to the exposure of the true culprit, Ferdinand Walsin Esterhazy. However, due to anti-Semitic influences, French military authorities hesitated to acknowledge their mistake. It wasn't until 1906 when the Supreme Court finally exonerated Dreyfus, reinstating him as a Major in the army. He later served in World War I and passed away in 1935. Observing these injustices, Herzl recognized the urgent necessity for a homeland where Jews could live free from persecution.[65]

In 1896, Herzl published his seminal work, "Der Judenstaat" (The Jewish State), wherein he articulated the necessity of a sovereign Jewish state as a solution to anti-Semitism. This groundbreaking manifesto laid the groundwork for the Zionist movement and propelled Herzl onto the international stage as its preeminent leader.[66]

First Zionist Congress (1897)

The widespread antisemitism and persecution of Jewish communities in late 19th and early 20th century Europe were major catalysts for the Zionist movement. Discrimination, violence, and pogroms fuelled the desire for a safe homeland. Theodor Herzl founded the Zionist newspaper Die Welt in Vienna, Austria-Hungary, and organized the historic First Zionist Congress in Basel, Switzerland, using his own resources in 1897.[67]

As president of the Congress, Herzl embarked on an intensive diplomatic campaign to garner support for a Jewish state. This included meetings with influential figures like Kaiser Wilhelm II and active involvement in international forums such as the Hague Peace Conference.[68] These efforts culminated in the establishment of the World Zionist Organization (WZO) during the Congress, with Herzl elected unanimously as its inaugural president. Leveraging his position, Herzl engaged with prominent Jewish figures and philanthropists, such as the Rothschilds and Maurice de Hirsch, emphasizing the urgent necessity for a Jewish homeland amidst escalating persecution.[69]

In 1898, Herzl set out on his inaugural voyage to Jerusalem, aiming to secure global acknowledgment for the Zionist movement. Despite his earnest endeavours, Herzl encountered formidable obstacles, including resistance from influential financiers and setbacks in negotiations with key figures such as Pope Pius X and British Colonial Secretary Joseph Chamberlain. Tragically, he passed away on July 3, 1904, before witnessing the realization of his profound vision.[70]

The Zionist Federation of Great Britain and Ireland (1899)

Formed after the inaugural Zionist Congress in Basel, Switzerland, in 1899, the Zionist Federation of Great Britain and Ireland (ZF) swiftly rose to prominence as a staunch proponent of Zionism and Israel within the United Kingdom. Its significance became notably pronounced through its instrumental role in championing the Balfour Declaration, a pivotal moment where Britain pledged support for establishing a "national home for the Jewish people" in Palestine. Today, serving as a unifying force, the ZF acts as an umbrella organization encompassing over 30 affiliated groups and boasting a membership exceeding 50,000 individuals. Aligned with the World Zionist Organization, the ZF extends its reach globally, amplifying its advocacy efforts on an international scale.[71]

Sykes-Picot Agreement (1916)

Amidst the chaos of World War I (1914 to 1918), as the Ottoman Empire teetered on the edge of collapse, the British and French seized the opportunity to assert their imperial ambitions in the Middle East.[72] The Sykes-Picot Agreement of 1916 was a secret treaty between the UK and France, with involvement from Russia and Italy, aiming to partition the Ottoman Empire. Negotiated by Mark Sykes and François Georges-Picot, it delineated British and French spheres of influence in the Middle East. The agreement allocated territories to each power, with the British gaining control over parts of Palestine, Jordan, and Iraq, and France over southeastern Turkey, Syria, and Lebanon. Russia retained control over Istanbul, the Bosphorus strait area, and four provinces in eastern Anatolia. Additionally, the agreement assigned Greece to administer Turkey's western coasts and Italy to govern the southwest region of Turkey.[73]

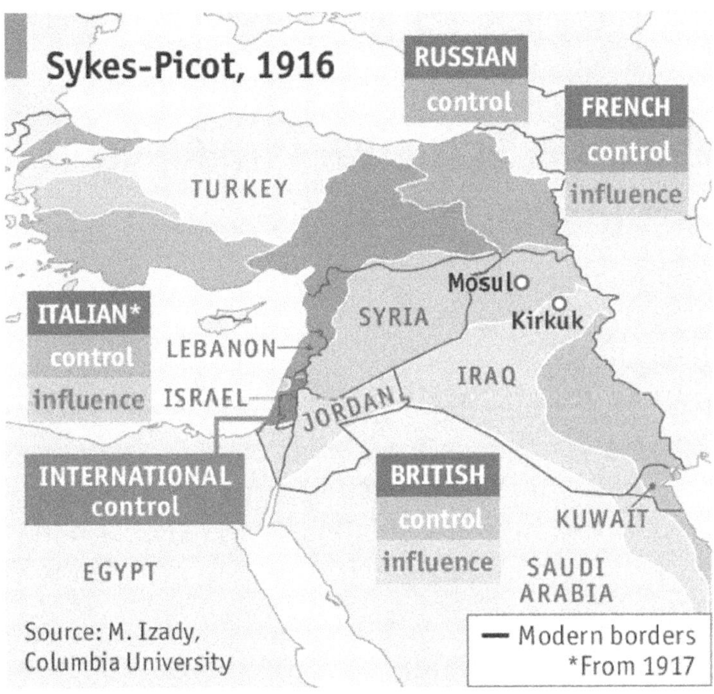

Figure 4. Sykes-Picot 1916 (The Economist, 2016)

In 1917, following the overthrow of Russian Tsar Nicholas II in a popular revolution, the Bolshevik communists, led by Vladimir Lenin, uncovered a copy of the Sykes-Picot agreement in the government's archives. Lenin's colleague, Leon Trotsky, then published the agreement in Izvestia newspaper on November 24, 1917, with the intention of revealing the great powers' plans to inherit the Ottoman Empire post-World War I. Lenin denounced the treaty as "the agreement of the colonial thieves," sparking a political scandal for Britain and France.[74]

The revelation of the agreement caused embarrassment for the British, uproar among Arabs who felt betrayed by the UK's reneging on promises of Arab independence. The aftermath of the agreement saw the emergence of new states and ongoing tensions, shaping the region's history for decades. Its impact continues to fuel resentment in the region, particularly among Arabs and Kurds who were denied independent states.[75]

The Balfour Declaration: A Turning Point in Zionist History (1917)

The Balfour Declaration, issued on November 2, 1917, by British Foreign Secretary Arthur James Balfour during World War I, marks a pivotal moment in Zionist history. This declaration expressed British support for the establishment of a "national home for the Jewish people" in Palestine, which was then part of the Ottoman Empire.[76]

The catalyst for the Balfour Declaration arose from discussions between British officials and prominent Zionist leaders, notably Chaim Weizmann, who later became Israel's first President. This declaration, conveyed in a letter to Lionel Walter Rothschild, a British banker and a prominent British Zionist leader, who was a member of the Rothschild family.[77]

While validating Zionist aspirations worldwide, also served British strategic interests in the Middle East. This included securing support from Jewish communities in the United States and Russia. Additionally, Britain aimed to establish a pro-British Jewish population in Palestine to safeguard the approaches to the Suez Canal in neighbouring Egypt.[78]

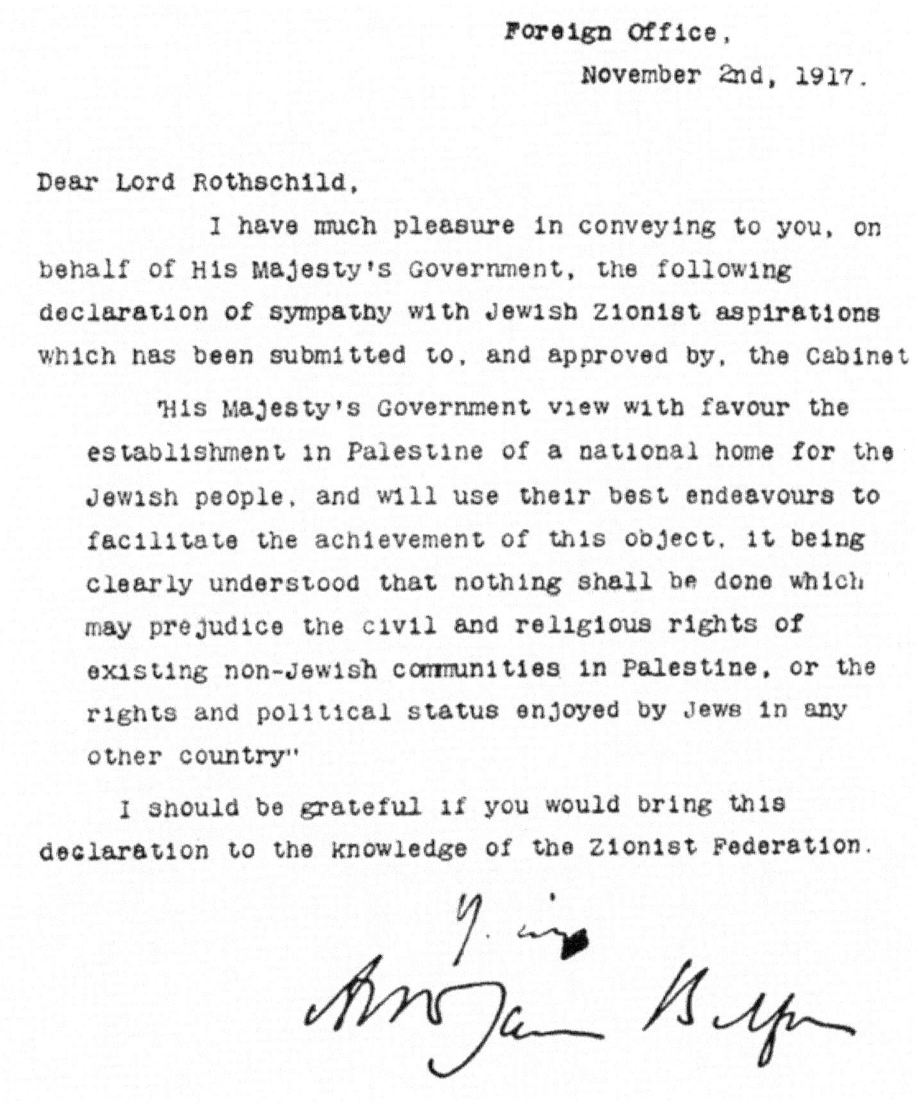

Foreign Office,

November 2nd, 1917.

Dear Lord Rothschild,

      I have much pleasure in conveying to you, on behalf of His Majesty's Government, the following declaration of sympathy with Jewish Zionist aspirations which has been submitted to, and approved by, the Cabinet

      "His Majesty's Government view with favour the establishment in Palestine of a national home for the Jewish people, and will use their best endeavours to facilitate the achievement of this object, it being clearly understood that nothing shall be done which may prejudice the civil and religious rights of existing non-Jewish communities in Palestine, or the rights and political status enjoyed by Jews in any other country"

      I should be grateful if you would bring this declaration to the knowledge of the Zionist Federation.

Figure 5. Balfour Declaration (Wiki commons, 2019)

However, the Balfour Declaration was not without controversy. It sparked opposition from Arab nationalists who viewed the establishment of a Jewish homeland as a threat to their own aspirations for self-determination. The ensuing tensions between Jewish and Arab communities in Palestine would later erupt into violent conflict, setting the stage for decades of strife in the region.[79]

The League of Nations Mandate (1920)

The League of Nations granted Britain the mandate to oversee Palestine following the collapse of the Ottoman Empire after World War I. The League of Nations was an intergovernmental organization founded on January 10, 1920, as a result of the Paris Peace Conference that ended World War I. It aimed to promote international cooperation, maintain peace and security, and prevent future conflicts.[80]

Based on Article 22 of the League of Nations Covenant and the San Remo Resolution, the mandate aimed to provide administrative guidance until the territories could govern independently. The mandate document included a commitment to realizing the principles outlined in the Balfour Declaration, thereby facilitating Jewish immigration and settlement in Palestine. This mandate, which also encompassed Transjordan after the Franco-Syrian War, initiated a period of nearly three decades during which Britain administered the region until 1948, culminating in the Israeli Declaration of Independence.[81]

During this period, Jewish immigration to Palestine increased, leading to tensions and riots primarily sparked by Arab opposition to Jewish immigration and land purchases in the region.[82]

Creation of the Haganah (1920)

The Haganah was a Jewish paramilitary organization that played a significant role in the defense of Jewish communities in British Mandate Palestine. Originally established to safeguard against local Arab attacks, it transformed into a key military force within the Jewish community as Israel's statehood approached in 1948. Post-independence, the Haganah formed the basis of the Israel Defense Forces (IDF).[83]

Jaffa riots (1921)

The Jaffa riots from May 1–7, 1921 were triggered by a May Day parade organized by the Jewish Communist Party, which called for the overthrow of British rule and the establishment of a "Soviet Palestine." The parade clashed with a rival socialist group's procession, leading to violence. The violence escalated into Arab attacks on Jews, followed by reprisals by Jews on Arabs. The rioting began in Jaffa but spread across the country, resulting in 47 Jewish and 48 Arab deaths, with many more wounded. The British authorities declared a state of emergency and intervened militarily.[84]

Arab leaders petitioned the League of Nations for independence and democracy noting that the Arab community contained sufficient educated and talented members to establish a stable representative democracy. In response to this, High Commissioner Sir Herbert

Samuel established an investigative commission, led by Sir Thomas Haycraft, Chief Justice of the Supreme Court in Palestine.[85]

The commission's report angered both Jews and Arabs: It placed the blame on the Arabs but stated that "Zionists were not doing enough to mitigate the Arabs' apprehensions." The report concluded that "the fundamental cause of the violence and the subsequent acts of violence was a feeling among the Arabs of discontent with, and hostility to, the Jews, due to political and economic causes, and connected with Jewish immigration."[86]

First official census of Palestine (1922)

The first official census of Palestine, conducted by British authorities in 1922, provides valuable insights into the demographic composition of the region at that time. The official census recorded a total population of 757,182 individuals, among them, 590,890 were Muslims, 83,794 were Jews, and 73,024 were Christians.[87]

In 1860, the population of Palestine was estimated at 411,000 individuals, predominantly Sunni Muslims, alongside significant minority groups including Christians, Shia Muslims, and Druze.[88]

Jewish Agency (1929)

The Jewish Agency, established in 1929, served as the official representative body of the Jewish community in Palestine during the British Mandate. It worked closely with the British authorities to advocate for Jewish interests and concerns, particularly regarding immigration, land development, and security. The Agency played a crucial role in promoting Jewish immigration to Palestine, facilitating settlement expansion through land acquisition and development projects. Additionally, it invested in education, healthcare, and cultural initiatives to strengthen the Jewish community and lay the groundwork for the future State of Israel.[89]

Palestine riots and Hebron Massacre (1929)

The 1929 Palestine riots, also known as the Buraq Uprising, were a series of demonstrations and riots that occurred in late August 1929. They originated from a longstanding dispute between Palestinian Arabs and Jews over access to the Western Wall in Jerusalem, escalating into widespread violence. The riots were fuelled by rumours that Jews were planning to seize control of the Temple Mount in Jerusalem. Tragically, the riots resulted in the loss of 133 Jewish lives and 110 Arab lives.[90]

The Nuremberg Laws (1935)

The Nuremberg Laws of 1935, enacted by the Nazi regime in Germany, were pivotal in institutionalizing anti-Semitic discrimination and racial segregation.

The Nuremberg Laws consisted of two main decrees. The Reich Citizenship Law stripped German Jews of their citizenship and classified them as "subjects" rather than citizens. It deprived them of many rights and protections under German law. The Law for the Protection of German Blood and German Honor prohibited marriage and sexual relations between Jews and non-Jews (often referred to as "Aryans"). It aimed to maintain the purity of German blood and prevent what the Nazis perceived as racial contamination. This law also restricted the employment of German women under the age of 45 in Jewish households.[91]

These laws paved the way for the systematic discrimination, marginalization, and eventual genocide of millions of Jews during the Holocaust.

Arab Revolt (1936)

The Arab Revolt of 1936-1939 was an uprising in Mandatory Palestine against British colonial rule and Jewish immigration. Led by the Arab Higher Committee (AHC), chaired by Haj Amin al-Husseini, the Grand Mufti of Jerusalem, it was fuelled by resentment towards Jewish settlers, economic disparities, and perceived British favouritism. British forces suppressed the revolt, imposing curfews, conducting military operations, and arresting Palestinian activists, leading to significant casualties and unrest. The revolt's legacy includes strained Arab-Jewish relations and policy changes like the White Paper of 1939, which limited Jewish immigration. It is seen as a precursor to later Arab-Israeli conflicts, shaping the region's political landscape.[92]

Peel Commission (1936-1937)

Amidst the tumult of the Arab Revolt, British government sought to address the conflict through the establishment of a royal commission of inquiry. Led by Lord Robert Peel, this commission embarked on a mission to investigate the roots of the Arab-Jewish strife and propose viable solutions.[93]

After extensive hearings and testimonies in Palestine, the Peel Commission unveiled its recommendations in July 1937. Central to its proposal was the idea of abolishing the Mandate and partitioning the land between Arab and Jewish populations. However, this vision came with significant territorial delineations and restrictions.

The allocation of land proposed by the commission was approximately as follows: the Jewish State would receive about 17% of the land, including the coastal plain from Mount Carmel to south of Be'er Tuvia, as well as the Jezreel Valley and parts of the Galilee. The Arab State would encompass approximately 75% of the land, including the hill regions, Judea and Samaria (also known as the West Bank), and the Negev desert. Around 8% of the land, including the area between Jaffa and Jerusalem, would remain under British mandate and international supervision. Notably, the commission suggested reunifying the Arab state with Transjordan, which had been separated in 1921.[94]

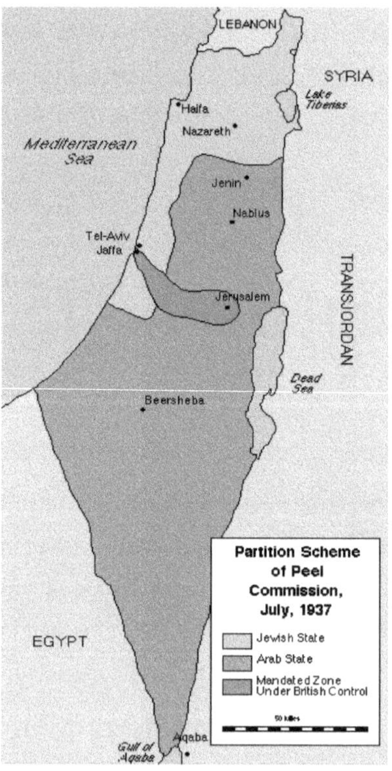

Figure 6. Peel Commission's partition plan (Embassy of Israel,2024)

The Peel Commission's partition plan, however, was met with skepticism and resistance from both Arab and Jewish communities. While it offered a diplomatic framework for addressing territorial disputes, it also highlighted the deep-seated divisions and historical grievances that continued to fuel conflict in Palestine. The plan was ultimately set aside, but the concept of partition was later revived and embraced by the United Nations in 1947.[95]

White Paper (1939)

The 1939 White Paper issued by the British government introduced stringent restrictions on Jewish immigration to Palestine, a move that sparked significant controversy, especially in light of the escalating Nazi persecution of Jews in Europe. With the Holocaust looming, the limited avenues for Jewish refugees to find sanctuary in Palestine exacerbated the humanitarian crisis.[96]

The White Paper severely limited Jewish immigration to Palestine, stating that only 75,000 Jews would be allowed to enter over a five-year period. The Zionist movement vehemently opposed the White Paper, viewing it as a betrayal of the earlier promises made in the Balfour Declaration, which had pledged British support for the establishment of a Jewish homeland in Palestine. The severe restrictions on immigration and land acquisition were seen as a direct impediment to the Zionist vision of creating a Jewish state. However, while the White Paper aimed to address Arab grievances and foster better relations between Jewish and Arab communities, it fell short of fully satisfying Arab demands. Arab leaders continued to call for an end to Jewish immigration and land acquisition, highlighting the deep-rooted tensions and conflicting aspirations in the region.[97]

Ultimately, the 1939 White Paper stands as a symbol of the complex and fraught political landscape of Mandatory Palestine, where competing interests and historical grievances collided, shaping the course of the Israeli-Palestinian conflict for decades to come.

World War-2 and Holocaust (1939-1945)

World War II was a global conflict of unprecedented scale and devastation. It began with Nazi Germany's invasion of Poland in September 1939, triggering a series of events that engulfed most of the world in war.

Key events of the war included Germany's rapid conquests in Europe through blitzkrieg tactics, the Battle of Britain in 1940 where the Royal Air Force repelled German air attacks, and the brutal conflict on the Eastern Front between Germany and the Soviet Union during Operation Barbarossa. In the Pacific, Japan's aggression led to the attack on Pearl Harbor on December 7, 1941, prompting the U.S. entry into the war.[98]

Amidst the chaos of war, the Holocaust unfolded, a systematic genocide orchestrated by Nazi Germany, resulting in the systematic murder of approximately six million Jews, along with millions of others deemed undesirable by the Nazis, including Roma, disabled individuals, Slavs, political dissidents, and others.[99]

The Holocaust occurred due to a combination of factors, including deep-rooted anti-Semitic beliefs prevalent in Europe for centuries, exacerbated by economic and social instability. Hitler, apart from being an anti-Semite, was a fervent believer of "Jewish-Bolshevism," alleging Jewish involvement in the spread of socialism and Germany's defeat in World War I. Hitler propagated the notion that Jews aimed to establish socialism in Germany and annihilate the Aryan race. This belief laid the groundwork for the Holocaust, as Hitler saw genocide as necessary to protect Germany from perceived threats.[100] The Holocaust remains a harrowing testament to the depths of human depravity and the consequences of unchecked hatred and prejudice.

UN Partition Plan Resolution-181 (1947)

Following World War II, the situation in Palestine became increasingly volatile. In February 1947, Britain announced its intention to terminate the Mandate, leading to escalating tensions.[101]

In May 1947, the United Nations assumed responsibility for the Palestine issue and formed the Special Committee on Palestine (UNSCOP). This committee proposed recommendations aimed at transitioning Palestine to independence. These recommendations included maintaining the status quo on holy sites and addressing the postwar Jewish refugee problem. UNSCOP presented two plans: a Plan of Partition with Economic Union and a Federal State Solution. The UN General Assembly established an Ad Hoc Committee to review UNSCOP's report, attended by representatives from the Arab Higher Committee and the Jewish Agency. While the Arab Higher Committee rejected both UNSCOP proposals, the Jewish Agency accepted the partition plan but sought revisions, particularly regarding the inclusion of Jerusalem and the western Galilee in the Jewish state. The proposed Jewish state would encompass 56 percent of Mandate Palestine, while the Arab state would cover 43 percent. [102]

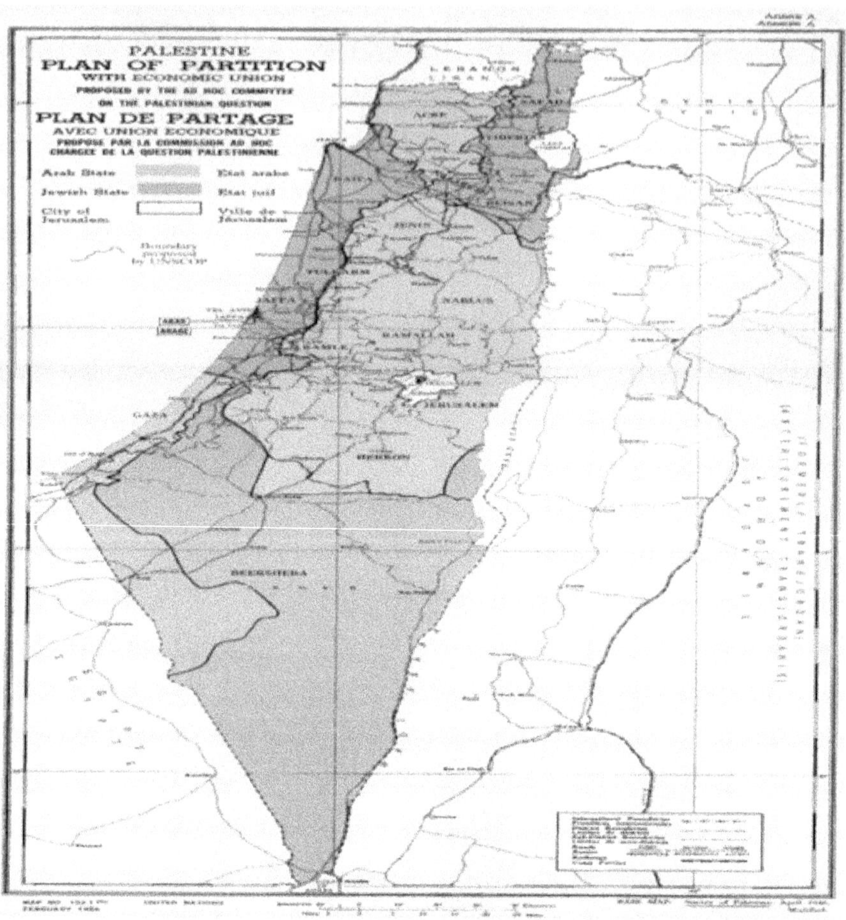

Figure 7. UN Partition Plan (wikipedia,2013)

The UN vote on the partition resolution was delayed to allow for extensive lobbying efforts. Finally, on November 29, 1947, the resolution was adopted with 33 votes in favour, 13 against, and 10 abstentions. [103]

Overall, the reactions of Arabs and Jews to the UN's acceptance of partition were diverse. Many Arab leaders and communities rejected the plan, considering it unjust and detrimental to their interests. On the other hand, Jewish reactions varied depending on ideological and political affiliations. Zionist leaders and supporters generally welcomed the partition plan as a significant step towards the establishment of a Jewish homeland. [104]

Declaration of the State of Israel and Israel's War of Independence (1948)

The Arab-Israeli War, known as the War of Independence in Israel and the Nakba (meaning "catastrophe" in Arabic), was a pivotal moment in Middle Eastern history. On May 14, 1948, David Ben-Gurion, the head of the Jewish Agency, declared the establishment of the State of Israel. Almost immediately, Arab states, including Egypt, Jordan, Syria, Iraq, and others, swiftly intervened militarily to prevent the establishment of Israel. They viewed the creation of Israel as a violation of Arab rights and sovereignty in Palestine. [105]

The war lasted for approximately one year and resulted in significant loss of life and displacement of populations. Despite being outnumbered and outgunned, Israeli forces managed to repel the Arab armies and even expanded their territory beyond the borders proposed by the UN partition plan. By the war's end, Israel controlled 78% of Mandatory Palestine, and at least 15,000 Arabs were killed. Around 500 Arab-majority towns and villages were depopulated or destroyed during the 1948 Arab-Israeli War. Approximately 750,000 Palestinians were expelled or fled to surrounding Arab countries.[106]

The war ended in 1949 with a series of armistice agreements between Israel and its Arab neighbours. These agreements established the Green Line, or armistice line, dividing Israeli-controlled territory from Arab-held areas like the West Bank and Gaza. To monitor the ceasefire, the UN set up supervisory agencies.[107] Additionally, the Tripartite Declaration of 1950, signed by the US, UK, and France, pledged to prevent violations, promote peace, and discourage an arms race in the region.[108]

The Institute for Intelligence and Special Operations, known as Mossad (1949)

Mossad stands as the national intelligence agency of the State of Israel. Operating in tandem with Aman (military intelligence) and Shin Bet (internal security), Mossad holds a pivotal position within the Israeli Intelligence Community.

Established on December 13, 1949, at the behest of Prime Minister David Ben-Gurion, Mossad emerged as a formidable force in intelligence gathering, covert operations, and counterterrorism. Mossad operates with unparalleled autonomy, reporting directly to the Prime Minister rather than to the Knesset. This unique arrangement has earned Mossad the label of a "deep state," reflecting its formidable influence within Israel's power structure.[109]

Law of Return (1950)

The Law of Return, enacted by the Israeli Knesset (Unicameral parliament) on July 5, 1950, stands as a pivotal piece of legislation governing Jewish immigration to Israel. Rooted in the Zionist ideology, this law is emblematic of Israel's identity as a Jewish state, offering a legal structure to streamline Jewish immigration. Initially, its scope was primarily defined by Orthodox interpretations of Jewish law, granting the right of return to those recognized as Jewish. However, significant amendments in 1970 broadened its application, extending eligibility to individuals with at least one

Jewish grandparent and to those married to Jews, regardless of their own religious beliefs.[110]

AIPAC: Shaping U.S. – Israel Relations (1951)

Established in 1951, the American Israel Public Affairs Committee (AIPAC) has risen to prominence as a leading lobbying organization in the United States, exerting significant influence on matters pertaining to Israel and the Middle East. Through strategic advocacy and grassroots mobilization, AIPAC has played a pivotal role in shaping U.S. foreign policy and strengthening the bond between the United States and Israel.[111]

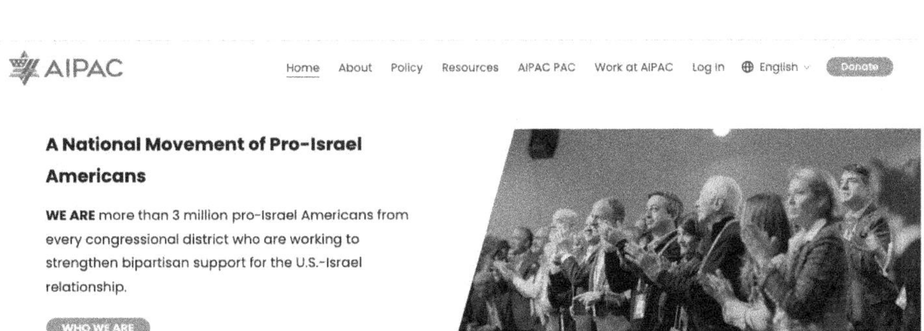

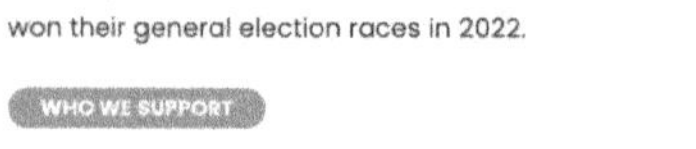

Figure 8. AIPAC Website (AIPAC,2024)

Suez Crisis (1956)

The Suez Crisis of 1956 was triggered by Egyptian President Gamal Abdel Nasser's nationalization of the Suez Canal, prompting a joint invasion by Israel, Britain, and France. Despite expectations of an easy victory, they faced a humiliating retreat as the US and Soviet Union opposed their actions. This marked the end of European imperialism and heralded a new international order. The crisis had far-reaching consequences for Britain, France, the Arab world, Israel, and the United States.[112]

The Suez Canal, completed in 1869, revolutionized global navigation by providing a shortcut from Europe to Asia and held strategic importance for Britain's trade and military efforts. However, by 1956, Britain's influence was waning, and anti-colonial sentiments were rising in Egypt. When Nasser nationalized the Canal in 1956 to fund the Aswan Dam project, this move triggered a swift and dramatic response from Britain, France, and Israel. In a covert operation, they conspired to reclaim the Canal, remove Nasser from power, and assert their dominance in the region. International condemnation forced Britain and France to withdraw. The crisis underscored the US and Soviet Union's ascendancy and emboldened Arab nationalism, cementing Nasser's role as a symbol of resistance.[113]

JFK: Leadership, Challenges, and Nuclear Diplomacy (1961-1963)

US President John F. Kennedy's presidency, from January 20, 1961, until his assassination on November 22, 1963, was marked by significant challenges and pivotal events. He faced the Cuban Missile Crisis, where he averted nuclear conflict with the Soviet Union, and he supported the civil rights movement, advancing racial equality in the U.S.[114]

Internationally, Kennedy's leadership was characterized by his commitment to diplomacy and non-proliferation efforts. Concerned about Israel's nuclear program, he pushed for inspections at Israel's Dimona Nuclear facility to prevent nuclear weapons development. Through diplomatic pressure, high-level discussions, and surveillance, Kennedy sought to curb Israeli nuclear activity, fearing regional instability and Soviet influence. In 1961, Kennedy met with Israeli Prime Minister David Ben-Gurion and pressed him on the issue of inspecting Israel's nuclear facility at Dimona. However, the inspections that were allowed were not rigorous and did not reveal the true nature of Israel's nuclear weapons program.[115] In Jul 1963, Kennedy sent a strongly worded telegram to Israeli Prime Minister Levi Eshkol, warning that U.S. support for Israel could be "seriously jeopardized" if Israel did not allow periodic inspections of Dimona. However, it was only after President Kennedy's assassination in November 1963 that Israel fulfilled this pledge in 1964.[116]

The Birth of the Palestinian Liberation Organization (1964)

The Palestinian Liberation Organization (PLO) emerged in 1964 during an Arab League Summit in Cairo, Egypt, with the aim of representing Palestinian aspirations for self-determination, independence, and the establishment of a Palestinian state. Initially led by Ahmed Shukeiri, the PLO has historically encompassed various Palestinian political factions, including nationalist, socialist, and Islamist groups. Its main goals include the recognition of Palestinian statehood, the right of return for Palestinian refugees, and the establishment of East Jerusalem as the capital of a future Palestinian state.[117]

One of the most notable factions within the PLO is Fatah, founded in 1959 by Yassir Arafat and Khalīl al-Wazīr (Abū Jihād). It aimed to liberate Palestine from Israeli control through guerrilla warfare. Arafat led Fatah until his death in 2004. Following his tenure, Mahmoud Abbas succeeded him, continuing the organization's pursuit of Palestinian rights and statehood. The PLO has engaged in various forms of resistance against Israeli occupation, including armed struggle, diplomatic efforts, and grassroots activism. Over the years, the PLO has been involved in numerous negotiations and peace processes with Israel, including the Oslo Accords in the 1990s.[118]

Operation Diamond: Mossad's Defection Mission (1966)

Operation Diamond in 1966 marked a remarkable chapter in the history of espionage and covert operations, as Mossad orchestrated the defection of Iraqi Air Force MiG-21 pilot, Capt. Munir Redfa, an Assyrian Christian, to Israel. The MiG-21, a crucial Soviet fighter jet introduced in 1959, played a vital role during the Cold War as a supersonic interceptor and air superiority fighter, reaching speeds beyond Mach 2. Its straightforward design, adaptability, and various models made it a key asset for numerous air forces worldwide. Capt. Munir Redfa 's defection was facilitated by Mossad, with the Israeli government offering him $1 million, Israeli citizenship, and full-time employment. His condition of smuggling his family out of Iraq was accepted.[119]

The MiG-21 provided invaluable intelligence to the Israeli Air Force, allowing them to evaluate its strengths and weaknesses, which proved crucial in subsequent Arab-Israeli conflicts from 1967 to 1973. In January 1968, Israel loaned the aircraft to the United States for further evaluation under the Have Donut program at Area 51, contributing to a deeper understanding of Soviet military technology and tactics during the Cold War era.[120]

Six-Day War: A Turning Point in Middle Eastern History (1967)

The Six-Day War was a significant conflict that took place between June 5th and 10th, 1967 between Israel and the neighbouring states of Egypt, Jordan, and Syria. Israel launched a pre-emptive strike against Egypt, targeting its air force to gain air superiority. This move was prompted by the closure of the Straits of Tiran by Egypt and the buildup of Arab forces along Israel's borders.[121]

In a stunning display of military prowess, Israel swiftly defeated the combined forces of Egypt, Jordan, and Syria, capturing the Sinai Peninsula and Gaza Strip from Egypt, the West Bank from Jordan, and the Golan Heights from Syria. The war ended on June 10, 1967, after a United Nations-brokered ceasefire.

The war exacted a heavy toll in terms of human lives. Over 20,000 Arab casualties were reported, while Israel suffered almost 1,000 fatalities. Civilian casualties included 20 Israeli civilians killed in airstrikes on Jerusalem by Arab forces. Additionally, 15 UN peacekeepers lost their lives due to Israeli strikes in the Sinai at the war's onset.[122]

Furthermore, the USS Liberty incident claimed the lives of 34 US personnel. This tragic event occurred when Israeli air forces attacked the USS Liberty, a United States Navy technical research ship, leading to significant loss of life and raising questions about the circumstances surrounding the attack.[123]

The outcome of the Six-Day War had profound implications for the region. Israel's victory reshaped the geopolitical landscape of the Middle East, significantly expanding its territory and influence. The war also led to the displacement of hundreds of thousands of Palestinians, contributing to the ongoing Israeli-Palestinian conflict. Additionally, it heightened tensions between Israel and its Arab neighbours, setting the stage for further conflicts in the years to come.

Munich Olympics Massacre (1972)

The 1972 Olympic Summer Games in Munich, Germany, were marred by a tragic terrorist attack perpetrated by eight members of the Palestinian militant organization Black September. They infiltrated the Olympic Village, killed two members of the Israeli Olympic team, and took nine others hostage, situation lasted for almost 24 hours. The terrorists demanded the release of Palestinian prisoners held in Israeli jails, as well as the imprisoned founders of the Red Army Faction in West Germany.[124]

Negotiations between the terrorists and German authorities failed, and a botched rescue attempt at a nearby airfield led to the deaths of all nine remaining hostages, as well as five terrorists and one German police officer. The Munich massacre, as it came to be known, shocked the world and led to significant changes in security protocols for future Olympic Games. It was a tragic event that highlighted the vulnerability of such large-scale international events to terrorism.[125]

Yom Kippur War, also known as the October War (1973)

The 1973 Yom Kippur War, also known as the October War, was a pivotal event in the ongoing Arab Israeli conflict with significant global implications. Egypt and Syria launched a surprise attack on Israel during Yom Kippur, the holiest day in Judaism. caught Israel off guard, challenging its perceived military invincibility. This demonstrated that Arab nations were capable of launching coordinated offensives against Israel.[126]

The conflict quickly escalated with the United States backing Israel and the Soviet Union supporting Arab states. This superpower involvement heightened tensions between the Cold War rivals and added an additional layer of complexity to the regional conflict. The involvement of Arab oil-producing nations in the conflict led to oil embargoes against countries supporting Israel, primarily the United States. This had significant economic implications globally, with oil prices skyrocketing and affecting economies worldwide. The war eventually ended in a ceasefire, prompting diplomatic efforts to resolve the conflict. The ceasefire led to negotiations and agreements such as the 1979 Camp David Accords between Israel and Egypt such as Israel eventually withdrew from the Sinai Peninsula which marked a significant step towards peace in the region.[127]

The Yom Kippur War prompted Israel to reassess its military strategy and leadership. It led to changes in defense policies and military preparedness to prevent future surprise attacks.

Henry Kissinger: A Complex Figure in Global Politics (1973)

Henry Alfred Kissinger was a highly influential Jewish American in diplomacy and politics, renowned for his roles as the United States Secretary of State and National Security Advisor under Presidents Richard Nixon and Gerald Ford from 1969 to 1977. Born in Germany in 1923, Kissinger's family fled Nazi persecution, and he later served in the U.S. Army during World War II. Many scholars, including Kissinger's biographer Walter Isaacson, have argued that his experiences influenced the formation of his realist approach to foreign policy.[128]

Kissinger played a pivotal role in Middle East diplomacy as US Secretary of State (1973-1977), particularly during and aftermath of the 1973 Arab Israeli War (Yom Kippur War). He pushed back against the Pentagon's attempts to delay the shipment of arms to Israel, rushing through weapons that helped the Israeli army reverse early losses and reach within 100 km of Cairo. He engaged in shuttle diplomacy between Egypt, Israel, and other Arab states, culminating in the 1974 disengagement agreements between Israel and Egypt, as well as between Israel and Syria.[129]

Kissinger aimed to manage rather than resolve the Israeli-Arab conflict, seeking incremental steps and temporary agreements to buy time for eventual reconciliation. He prioritized bolstering Israel's security and countering Soviet influence overachieving lasting peace. While his diplomacy laid groundwork for future agreements, his neglect of the Israeli-Palestinian issue has been criticized for exacerbating regional turmoil.[130]

The Lebanese Civil War (1975)

The Lebanese Civil War, a protracted and multifaceted armed conflict, unfolded from 1975 to 1990, leaving an indelible mark on Lebanon's history and society. Characterized by sectarian strife, foreign intervention, and shifting alliances, the war resulted in an estimated 150,000 fatalities and the displacement of nearly one million people. Israel formed alliances with various Lebanese factions, primarily Maronite Christian groups, based on shared opposition to the PLO.[131]

The country's parliamentary system, established under French mandate, favoured Christians, exacerbating tensions with Lebanon's Muslim Majority. In 1975, Muslims and leftists aligned with the PLO sought greater political influence, leading to fierce clashes with Christians aiming to maintain their dominance.[132]

Advocates: 'Self-Determination' for Palestinians (1978)

"The Advocates," a public television program, convened on June 6, 1978, to discuss whether the United States should support "self-determination" for Palestinians in a Middle East peace settlement. Moderated by Marilyn Berger, the panel featured Ben Nitay, an Economic Consultant (later known as Benjamin Netanyahu), who would go on to become Israel's longest-serving leader and reshape the country in his image.[133]

Netanyahu was born in 1949 in Tel Aviv. His father, Benzion Netanyahu, was a historian and Zionist activist renowned for his expertise in the golden age of Jewish culture in Spain, a period marked by the flourishing of Jewish life. Netanyahu's grandfather, Nathan Mileikowsky, was a prominent rabbi and Zionist writer.

Raised in Jerusalem and Philadelphia, Netanyahu returned to Israel in 1967 to join the IDF, where he excelled as a team leader in the elite Sayeret Matkal special forces, achieving the rank of captain before being honourably discharged. After graduating from the Massachusetts Institute of Technology, Netanyahu became an economic consultant for the Boston Consulting Group. He moved back to Israel in 1978 to found the Yonatan Netanyahu Anti-Terror Institute.[134]

Interviewer: PLO state is a deadly danger to world peace because it is the surest guarantee of increased terrorism and war, however noble the idea may sound. I call that as my first witness, Mr. Benjamin Netanyahu. Thank you, Mr. Netanyahu. Is the issue of self-determination the core of the conflict in the Middle East?

Benjamin Netanyahu: No, I don't believe it is. The real core of the conflict is the unfortunate Arab refusal to accept the State of Israel. For 20 years, the Arabs had both the West Bank and the Gaza Strip, and if self-determination was the core of the conflict, they could have easily established a Palestinian state then, but they didn't.

Interviewer: When did the issue arise then?

Benjamin Netanyahu: For 20 years, we didn't hear a word about self-determination. What we did hear was about driving the Jews into the sea. After 1967, under the leadership of the PLO, the strategy shifted to adopting a moderate dressed-up slogan which now talked in terms of first a secular democratic state and then replaced it with Palestinian self-determination.

Interviewer: Do the Palestinians have a right to a separate state?

Benjamin Netanyahu: No, I don't think they do. It's quite instructive that the Palestinians who are invoking the right of self-determination define themselves as part of the Arab nation. Also, there already exists a Palestinian state, Jordan, where 60 percent of the population is Palestinian.

Interviewer: What should be done with the Palestinians on the West Bank?

Benjamin Netanyahu: The Palestinians in the West Bank should be offered full human and civil rights, similar to what Arabs living in Israel have. I'm all in favor of offering them the same rights in a final peace agreement.

Interviewer: Do you sincerely hope for peace in the Middle East?

Benjamin Netanyahu: Yes, nobody wants peace more than Israel. But the stumbling block to the road for peace is the demand for a PLO state, which will mean more violence in the Middle East. I sincerely believe if this demand is abandoned, we can have real and genuine peace.

Interviewer: Mr. Netanyahu, you've mentioned that Palestinians on the West Bank and Gaza Strip would enjoy full human rights. How is that compatible with the presence of Israeli forces in their midst?

Benjamin Netanyahu: The Arabs living in Israel enjoy full human rights, including the right to vote. Similarly, in the West Bank and Gaza, once negotiations end, there is no reason why these Arabs won't have full human rights and the right to vote, whether under Jordanian or Israeli citizenship.

Interviewer: Does Israel accept that the people in the West Bank and Gaza Strip have the right to vote on their future?

Benjamin Netanyahu: Yes, in the event of continued negotiation, I'm sure these people will have the right to vote, whether under Jordanian or Israeli citizenship or any other arrangement.

Interviewer: Mr. Netanyahu, does the fact that Israel is dependent on the U.S. trouble you?

Benjamin Netanyahu: Israel is perhaps the only ally of the U.S. in the Middle East that has taken care of itself so far. It's not a one-way street; Israel provides the U.S. with stability and democracy in the region.

Interviewer: Given demographic predictions, does this challenge the foundations of Israel as a Jewish state?

Benjamin Netanyahu: No, the latest figures show a decrease in the Arab birthrate. Israel doesn't reject Palestinians or Arabs living in its midst; they are part of Israeli citizens and should have the right to multiply as they wish.

Interviewer: Since the subject is what should the United States do, could you summarize why Europe and the United States should oppose the creation of a PLO state?

Benjamin Netanyahu: The United States should oppose the creation of a Palestinian state because it is unjust to demand it at the expense of the only Jewish state. It will also defeat the hopes of moderate Palestinians who genuinely want peace with Israel.

Interviewer: As someone who believes in democracy, do you believe that Israel can continue as a garrison state and still remain at the Balearic States?

Benjamin Netanyahu: Israel does not intend to remain a garrison state. Israel wants to live in peace and security. If that involves maintaining military guarantees against those who seek our destruction, then yes, we will fight for our survival.

Interviewer: Thank you, Mr. Netanyahu, for your insights.

Camp David Accords (1978)

Following the Arab Israeli War, Secretary of State Henry Kissinger's diplomacy played a crucial role in laying the groundwork for the historic 1978 Camp David Accords. He successfully persuaded Israel and Egypt to engage in direct talks and make significant concessions in pursuit of peace.[135]

The Camp David Accords represented a momentous diplomatic achievement, consisting of two political agreements signed by Egyptian President Anwar Sadat and Israeli Prime Minister Menachem Begin on September 17, 1978. These accords emerged after twelve days of secretive negotiations at Camp David, the presidential retreat in Maryland, with President Jimmy Carter serving as a pivotal mediator.[136]

The signing ceremony occurred at the White House, where Sadat and Begin formally endorsed two framework agreements. The initial framework, "A Framework for Peace in the Middle East," focused on the Palestinian territories and was developed without Palestinian participation. Consequently, it faced criticism from the United Nations for its exclusionary approach. Notably, the second framework, titled "A Framework for the Conclusion of a Peace Treaty between Egypt and Israel," laid the foundation for the historic 1979 Egypt-Israel peace treaty. Their dedication to peace efforts garnered international recognition, leading to Sadat and Begin jointly receiving the Nobel Peace Prize in 1978.[137].

Iran-Iraq War (1980-1988)

The Iran-Iraq War was a prolonged and devastating conflict between Iran and Iraq, marked by extensive casualties and economic destruction. Initiated by Iraqi President Saddam Hussein's invasion of Iran on September 22, 1980, the war aimed to capitalize on Iran's post-revolutionary instability and gain control over the disputed, oil-rich Khuzestan region.[138]

The conflict featured brutal trench warfare, widespread use of chemical weapons, and attacks on civilian areas, resulting in approximately one million deaths on both sides. The economic toll was severe, with significant damage to oil facilities and infrastructure. International involvement was complex, with the United States, the Soviet Union, and various Arab states providing support to Iraq, while Iran largely relied on its resources.[139]

Despite early advances by Iraq, the war became a stalemate, with neither side achieving a decisive victory. It officially ended on August 20, 1988, following UN Resolution 598, which called for a ceasefire and a return to pre-war boundaries. The war left deep scars, significantly impacting regional geopolitics and contributing to future conflicts.[140]

Moral Majority (1979)

The Moral Majority was a prominent American political organization founded in 1979 by Rev. Jerry Falwell (1933–2007) an American evangelical Christian pastor, televangelist, and conservative political activist along with other conservative leaders, marking a significant moment in Christian Zionism. This occurred nearly a century after William Hechler the British Anglican priest, theologian, and Christian Zionist, offered to rally Christian support for a Jewish state to Theodor Herzl.[141]

In 1980, Falwell, who ran a television ministry that reached millions of viewers, said of Israel: "I firmly believe God has blessed America because America has blessed the Jew. If this nation wants her fields to remain white with grain, her scientific achievements to remain notable, and her freedom to remain intact, America must continue to stand with Israel." It played a pivotal role in securing Ronald Reagan's victory in the 1980 elections, being credited with providing him the winning edge. One of its key founding principles was unwavering "support for Israel and Jewish people everywhere."[142]

While the Moral Majority disbanded in the late 1989, its legacy continues to influence conservative politics in the United States, particularly in the realm of social and cultural issues.[143]

Operation Opera, also known as Operation Babylon (1981)

Operation Opera remains a pivotal event in the history of the Middle East, particularly in the context of regional security and nuclear proliferation concerns. On June 7, 1981, the Israeli Air Force (IAF) executed a meticulously planned airstrike, targeting an unfinished nuclear reactor located near Baghdad, Iraq. The strike was a pre-emptive measure aimed at thwarting Iraq's ambitions to develop nuclear weapons, which were perceived as a direct threat to Israel's security.[144]

The roots of Operation Opera can be traced back to Iraq's efforts to acquire nuclear capabilities in the 1970s. In 1976, Iraq purchased an Osiris-class nuclear reactor from France, ostensibly for peaceful scientific research. However, Israel viewed this acquisition with suspicion, fearing that Iraq's true intention was to develop nuclear weapons that could potentially escalate the ongoing Arab Israeli conflict. Before the strike, Mossad operatives carried out the assassination of Yehia El-Mashad, an Egyptian nuclear scientist, in a Paris hotel on June 14, 1980. El-Mashad had been overseeing Iraq's nuclear program during the late 1970s and early 1980s, playing a pivotal role in the construction of the Osirak reactor.[145]

In 1981, Prime Minister Menachem Begin greenlit Operation Opera, an Israeli Air Force strike on Iraq's Osirak reactor to pre-empt its nuclear threat. Despite global criticism, Israel justified the attack as self-defence. Operation Opera introduced the Begin Doctrine, underscoring Israel's resolve to thwart hostile states from obtaining weapons of mass destruction.[146]

First Lebanon War (1982)

The 1982 Lebanon War stands as a pivotal moment in the complex tapestry of Middle Eastern conflicts, leaving a lasting impact on the region's political landscape. Initiated by Israel's invasion of southern Lebanon on June 6, 1982, the war was a response to escalating hostilities between the Palestine Liberation Organization (PLO) and the Israeli military, marked by a series of deadly attacks and counterattacks along the border.[147]

The war quickly escalated, with Israeli forces, aided by Maronites (a Syriac Christian ethnoreligious group) and the separatist group

Free Lebanon State, advancing towards Beirut, the capital of Lebanon. In August 1982, under intense international pressure, Israel and the PLO agreed to a ceasefire mediated by the United States. As part of the ceasefire agreement, the PLO agreed to evacuate its forces from Lebanon, and a multinational peacekeeping force, including US, French, and Italian troops, was deployed to oversee the evacuation.[148]

Israel's objectives in the war transcended merely eliminating the PLO presence; they aimed to diminish Syrian influence in Lebanon and install a pro-Israeli Christian government led by President Bachir Gemayel. Menachem Begin pledged a treaty promising "forty years of peace" for Israel.[149]

Sabra and Shatila massacre (1982)

Lebanese President Bachir Gemayel was assassinated on September 14, 1982, just three weeks after his election as President of the Lebanese Republic. The bomb explosion occurred at the headquarters of the Lebanese Christian Phalangist Party in east Beirut. The perpetrator, Habib Shartouni, a member of the Syrian Social Nationalist Party (SSNP), planted the bomb in an apartment above Gemayel's room. Shartouni confessed to the assassination, citing his belief that Gemayel had "sold the country to Israel" as his motive.[150]

Gemayel's assassination had far-reaching consequences, including the "punitive" massacre of civilians in the Sabra and Chatila refugee camps on the night of September 17 to 18, resulted in a death toll estimated between 2,000-3,500 civilians. The massacre was carried out by a right-wing Lebanese Christian militia, the

Phalange, in coordination with the Israeli army during Israel's invasion of Lebanon. The victims, including Palestinian refugees and Lebanese civilians, endured horrific acts of slaughter, mutilation, rape, and mass graves over a period of 43 hours.[151] Despite the United Nations General Assembly declaring the massacre an "act of genocide," no Lebanese or Israeli fighter or official was punished for the crimes committed. The massacre remains a traumatic event in Palestinian history, commemorated annually.[152]

Zionism in the Age of the Dictators (1983)

"Zionism in the Age of the Dictators" is a 1983 work by Jewish – American author Lenni Brenner, prominent civil rights movement activist and vocal opponent of the Vietnam War. The book examines the controversial topic of Zionist collaboration with Nazi Germany before and during World War II.

The synopsis of the book states: "In 1933 the German Zionist Federation sought Hitler s patronage: "Zionism hopes to be able to win the collaboration even of a government fundamentally hostile to Jews.... Boycott propaganda... currently being carried on against Germany... is in essence un-Zionist." Zionism became the only other legal political movement in the Nazi Reich. That same year, the World Zionist Organization (WZO) made the Ha'avara (Transfer) Agreement, undermining the boycott against Nazi Germany. German Jewish emigrants to Palestine had to buy Nazi goods that the WZO sold in the Middle East. In 1937 the Haganah (later the Israeli army) sent an agent to Berlin. They would provide spy intelligence if the Nazis further eased the monetary regulations for emigrants to Palestine. The Zionist-Revisionist movement (today the ruling Likud Party) set up a detachment at Mussolini's naval academy. He personally reviewed them in 1936. They wanted him to replace Britain as Zionism s patron. In 1941, the Fighters for the Freedom of Israel (later Likudniks) told the Nazis that they wanted a "Jewish state on a national and totalitarian basis, bound by a treaty with the German Reich," and offered "to actively take part in the war on Germany s side." This is the sordid history documented in Lenni Brenner's Zionism in the Age of the Dictators."[153]

One of the key examples Brenner discusses is the Haavara Agreement, a pact between Nazi Germany and the Zionist Federation of Germany in 1933. This agreement facilitated the transfer of Jewish assets from Germany to Palestine, thereby enabling around 60,000 Jews to escape Nazi persecution while also supporting the Zionist project. However, Brenner's interpretation of these historical events is controversial and has been criticized by some scholars for its selective use of evidence and its portrayal of Zionist motives and actions. Overall, "Zionism in the Age of the Dictators" offers a provocative perspective on the complexities of Zionist politics and the dilemmas faced by Jewish leaders during a tumultuous period in history.[154]

Hezbollah, Party of God (1985)

The Lebanon War in 1982 paved the way for the emergence of Hezbollah, a Shiite Muslim political party and militant group which aligned ideologically with Iran's revolutionary principles. Initially formed to resist Israeli occupation, Hezbollah quickly became a significant player in Lebanese politics and society.[155]

Hezbollah's 1985 manifesto outlined its goals of expelling "the Americans, the French, and their allies definitively from Lebanon, putting an end to any colonialist entity on our land." From 1985 to 2000, it engaged in conflicts with the South Lebanon Army (SLA) and the Israel Defense Forces (IDF), seeking to safeguard Lebanese sovereignty. Over the years, Hezbollah expanded its activities beyond resisting Israeli occupation, particularly after Israel withdrew from Lebanon.[156]

The Hezbollah paramilitary wing is known as the Jihad Council, while its political wing is represented by the Loyalty to the Resistance Bloc party in the Lebanese Parliament. Hezbollah's military strength grew significantly, leading it to be described as a "state within a state." It receives support from Iran and Syria. While designated as a terrorist organization by several countries, it is considered a legitimate socio-political force by others, including Russia.[157]

US Senator Joe Biden's Diplomatic Dialogue (1986)

In February 1986, Israel's ambassador to the U.S., Meir Rosenne, met with Delaware Senator Joseph R. Biden Jr., who now serves as the President of the United States. This encounter took place two years before Biden's initial bid for the U.S. presidency in 1988. During the meeting, Senator Biden aimed to convey his unwavering support for Israel by proposing that the U.S. should prioritize Israel as "first but equal" in its relations with the Arab states.[158]

He asserted, "It's time we stop apologizing for our support for Israel in this body. There is no apology to be made. It is the best three-billion-dollar investment we make. Whether or not in Israel, the United States of America would have to invent an Israel to protect her interests in the region. People should understand by now, that should be crystal clear." At the end of the meeting, Biden repeated his commitment to Israel, adding that he "believes the United States did not do enough for the Jews during World War II". He ended by saying that we wouldn't be sorry if he were elected to the White House.[159] He criticized the Reagan administration's approach to U.S.-Israel relations and advocated for a more supportive stance towards Israel. Biden also voiced his anti-PLO position and criticized U.S. policy towards Saudi Arabia. This historical encounter sheds light on Biden's long-standing relationship with Israel and his perspective on Middle Eastern affairs.[160]

Mordechai Vanunu: Israel's Nuclear Whistleblower (1986)

Mordechai Vanunu, also known as John Crossman, is an Israeli former nuclear technician turned peace activist. In 1986, he disclosed details of Israel's nuclear weapons program to the British press due to his opposition to weapons of mass destruction. Following this revelation, Vanunu was lured to Italy by the Israeli intelligence agency Mossad, where he was drugged and abducted. He was then secretly transported to Israel and convicted in a trial held behind closed doors.[161]

Vanunu spent 18 years in prison, over 11 of which were in solitary confinement, despite no such punishment being specified in Israel's penal code. Upon his release in 2004, he faced numerous restrictions on his speech and movement, often being arrested for violating his parole terms by speaking to foreign journalists or attempting to leave Israel. Vanunu claims to have endured harsh treatment in prison, alleging it was exacerbated by his conversion to Christianity. He received the Right Livelihood Award in 1987 for his courage in exposing Israel's nuclear program.[162]

The First Intifada (1987)

The First Intifada, which began in 1987, marked a significant uprising by Palestinians against Israeli occupation in the West Bank and Gaza Strip. The protests, characterized by widespread civil disobedience, strikes, and demonstrations, aimed to challenge Israeli policies and demand Palestinian rights and self-determination. The Intifada, meaning "shaking off" in Arabic, lasted until the early 1990s and had a profound impact on the Israeli-Palestinian conflict, shaping future negotiations and resistance strategies.[163] The Israeli military response to the First Intifada was harsh, with Israeli forces killing more than 1,000 Palestinians and injuring more than 130,000. Tens of thousands more were imprisoned, and many were routinely tortured. The United Nations criticized Israel's use of lethal force, and the United States government under President Reagan condemned the violence.[164]

Hamas, Islamic Resistance Movement (1987)

Hamas (Islamic Resistance Movement) is a Palestinian Sunni Islamist political and military movement governing parts of the Israeli-occupied Gaza Strip. Hamas was founded by Palestinian imam, Sheikh Ahmed Yasin, and his aide Abdul Aziz al-Rantissi in 1987, after the outbreak of the First Intifada against the Israeli occupation. It emerged from 1973 Mujama al-Islamiya Islamic charity affiliated with the Muslim Brotherhood. Moreover, Hamas established a military wing known as the Izz al-Din al-Qassam Brigades, dedicated to engaging in armed conflict against Israel with the objective of liberating historic Palestine.[165]

The organization's founding charter, known as the Hamas Covenant, outlines its goals, which include the establishment of an Islamic state in historic Palestine and the liberation of all Palestinian territories from Israeli occupation. Hamas rejects the legitimacy of Israel and calls for the complete dismantlement of the state.[166]

Hamas operates primarily in the Gaza Strip, where it has established social service networks, educational institutions, and charitable organizations to provide support to Palestinians. Hamas has been a controversial and divisive organization, with some viewing it as a legitimate resistance movement fighting against Israeli occupation and others condemning it as a terrorist group responsible for violence.[167]

The Gulf War (1990-1991)

The Gulf War , also known as Operation Desert Storm, was triggered when Iraq, under Saddam Hussein, invaded and annexed Kuwait on August 2, 1990. Invasion of Kuwait in was primarily motivated by economic and political factors. Saddam viewed Kuwait as historically belonging to Iraq and resented Kuwait's economic policies, particularly its overproduction of oil, which drove down oil prices and harmed Iraq's economy. Iraq, grappling with significant debt from the Iran-Iraq War, saw Kuwait's oil-rich resources as a means to alleviate its financial struggles and bolster its regional influence.[168]

This invasion was met with widespread international condemnation and led to the formation of a coalition force led by the United States, under the auspices of the United Nations, to liberate Kuwait.[169]

The conflict began with a massive aerial bombing campaign on January 17, 1991, targeting Iraqi military and infrastructure, followed by a ground assault on February 24, 1991. The coalition, comprising forces from 35 nations, swiftly overwhelmed Iraqi forces, leading to the liberation of Kuwait within 100 hours of the ground campaign's commencement. The war officially ended on February 28, 1991, with a ceasefire declared by U.S. President George H.W. Bush. The Gulf War had significant geopolitical implications, including reinforcing U.S. presence in the Middle East and setting the stage for future conflicts.[170]

Madrid Peace Conference (1991)

The 1991 Madrid Peace Conference was a landmark diplomatic initiative aimed at resolving the Arab Israeli conflict. Co-sponsored by the United States and the Soviet Union, the conference gathered representatives from Israel, Arab states, and the Palestinians for bilateral and multilateral negotiations.[171]

Significantly, it was the first time that Israel engaged in peace talks with its Arab neighbours and the Palestinians. The Madrid conference laid the groundwork for subsequent peace efforts, including the Oslo Accords and the historic 1994 peace treaty between Israel and Jordan. Its importance lies in its role as a catalyst for dialogue and diplomacy in the quest for lasting peace in the Middle East.[172]

Oslo Accords (1993)

The Oslo Accords were a pair of transitional agreements signed by Israeli Prime Minister Yitzhak Rabin and PLO Chairman Yasser Arafat that were designed to establish a partnership for negotiating border disputes, creating Palestinian self-governance through the creation of the Palestinian Authority, and over time, the hope was this would lead to a peaceful solution to the conflict and a two-state solution. Negotiated secretly in Oslo, Norway, these accords marked the first direct, face-to-face talks between the two parties and were hailed as a historic breakthrough in the quest for peace in the region.[173]

The Oslo Accords consisted of two main agreements: Oslo I, officially known as the Declaration of Principles on Interim Self-Government Arrangements, and Oslo II, also known as the Israeli-Palestinian Interim Agreement. Oslo I outlined a framework for Palestinian self-rule in parts of the West Bank and Gaza Strip, while Oslo II provided further details on the implementation of Palestinian autonomy, including security arrangements, land transfers, and the establishment of the Palestinian Authority (PA) to govern the territories.[174]

The accords represented a significant shift in approach, as they moved away from the idea of immediate statehood for Palestinians and instead focused on interim arrangements leading to eventual Palestinian independence. They also marked a departure from the traditional Arab demand for Israel's withdrawal from all territories occupied in the 1967 Six-Day War, instead opting for a phased withdrawal.[175]

Jordan-Israel Peace Treaty (1994)

The 1994 Jordan-Israel Peace Treaty is a significant agreement between Jordan and Israel that normalized relations between the two nations. It recognized each other's sovereignty, established their international boundary, and fostered cooperation in security and economics. The treaty addressed historical disputes, with Jordan formally recognizing its loss of the West Bank and East Jerusalem in the 1967 Six-Day War.[176]

It established the Jordan River as the official border between the two nations. As the second Arab country to make peace with Israel, Jordan's willingness to engage diplomatically marked a pivotal moment in regional relations. The treaty has led to enhanced cooperation in various fields and serves as a symbol of the potential for dialogue and compromise to promote peace and stability in the Middle East.[177]

Assassination of Israeli PM Yitzhak Rabin (1995)

Yitzhak Rabin was a prominent Israeli statesman and military leader who served as the Prime Minister of Israel on two separate occasions, from 1974 to 1977 and from 1992 until his assassination in 1995. Born on March 1, 1922, in Jerusalem, Rabin played a significant role in shaping Israel's history through both his military service and his political leadership.[178]

Rabin's military career began during the pre-state period, when he joined the Haganah, the precursor to the Israel Defense Forces (IDF). He rose through the ranks and played key roles in Israel's War of Independence in 1948. Over the years, he held various high-ranking positions within the IDF, including Chief of Staff during the Six-Day War in 1967.In 1974, Rabin transitioned from his military career to politics, serving as Israel's Ambassador to the United States. He later held several ministerial positions in the Israeli government, including Minister of Labor and Minister of Defence.[179]

Rabin's most notable achievement came in 1993 when he, along with Palestinian leader Yasser Arafat and U.S. President Bill Clinton, signed the Oslo Accords, a historic agreement that aimed to achieve peace between Israel and the Palestinians. For his efforts in pursuing peace, Rabin was awarded the Nobel Peace Prize in 1994, along with Arafat and Israeli Foreign Minister Shimon Peres.[180]

Yitzhak Rabin, while addressing a peace rally in Tel Aviv on November 4, 1995, expressed hope for peace between Israelis and Palestinians, buoyed by the massive turnout of over 100,000 people, notably many young individuals. He urged Israelis to overcome their fears, confront the past, and embrace a future of harmony. Amidst the fervor of the rally, with teenagers brandishing Peace Now banners and splashing into fountains, Rabin's call to action echoed: "Let's not just sing about peace – let's make peace." Tragically, immediately after the rally, Rabin was assassinated by Yigal Amir, a nationalist extremist, cutting short his efforts for peace. Rabin's death dealt a severe blow to the peace process, with his government soon collapsing, and the dream of a lasting peace between Israelis and Palestinians fading away. His death shocked the nation and the world, highlighting the deep cultural and political divisions within Israel, reflecting a struggle between religious right-wing and secular left-wing forces.[181]

Benjamin Netanyahu: A Controversial Legacy (1996)

Netanyahu staked his political future on opposing the Oslo peace process, arguing that it would endanger Israel's security.[182] Netanyahu's political ideology is deeply influenced by Ze'ev Jabotinsky, a key figure in Revisionist Zionism. Revisionist Zionist ideology diverged from mainstream Zionist thought by advocating for territorial maximalism and a more assertive approach to achieving Jewish statehood. It emphasized the importance of Jewish sovereignty over the entire Land of Israel, including territories beyond what was designated by the mainstream Zionist movement. Revisionist Zionists rejected the idea of partitioning the land or compromising on Jewish rights to certain areas. They believed in the necessity of a strong Jewish military force to defend against external threats and to secure Jewish interests in the region. This ideology laid the groundwork for organizations like the Irgun, a militant Zionist organization that operated in the British Mandate of Palestine during the 1930s and 1940s, and later influenced the Likud party in Israel.[183]

The Likud party is a major Israeli political party that was established in 1973. It emerged as a coalition of several right-wing and nationalist parties, including Menachem Begin's Herut party, which was the political successor to the Irgun. The Likud party has been a dominant force in Israeli politics since its formation, advocating for a strong stance on security and a conservative approach to the Israeli-Palestinian conflict.[184]

During a demonstration in the summer of 1995 In July, Netanyahu participated in a mock funeral procession for Rabin, chanting "Death to Rabin" amidst signs branding him as a traitor for initiating Oslo Accord peace treaty. Critics claim that Netanyahu's rhetoric and actions contributed to the hostile environment that led to the assassination. Following Rabin's death, Netanyahu's political fortunes improved.[185]

In 1996, Shimon Peres, leader of the Labor party and Rabin's successor, called for elections to reaffirm public support for the Oslo peace process. Initially, it seemed promising, with Netanyahu's popularity diminished after Rabin's assassination. However, a series of suicide bombings before the May elections shifted support to Netanyahu. He capitalized on concerns about territorial compromise, portraying his opponent as weak and warning against dividing Jerusalem. With a narrow victory margin of less than 1%, Netanyahu became Israel's youngest prime minister, serving from 1996 to 1999.[186]

Second Intifada (2000)

The Second Intifada, also known as the Al-Aqsa Intifada, marked a tumultuous period of conflict and Palestinian resistance against Israeli occupation from late September 2000 to around 2005. Characterized by widespread protests, demonstrations, suicide bombings, and armed confrontations between Israeli security forces and Palestinian militants, it inflicted significant casualties on both sides, with roughly 3,000 Palestinians and 1,000 Israelis losing their lives between September 2000 and February 2005. This upheaval prompted Israel to construct the West Bank barrier and left a lasting impact on subsequent peace negotiations. Although officially declared over by 2005, its repercussions continue to reverberate through the region's political landscape.[187]

9/11: A Day of Terror That Forged a Stronger Bond Between Two Nations

On September 11, 2001, a series of coordinated terrorist attacks struck the United States. Hijackers associated with the extremist group al-Qaeda seized control of four commercial airliners, crashing two into the Twin Towers of the World Trade Center in New York City and one into the Pentagon near Washington, D.C. The fourth plane, United Airlines Flight 93, crashed into a field in Pennsylvania after passengers attempted to regain control from the hijackers.[188]

The attacks resulted in nearly 3,000 fatalities and caused extensive destruction, including the complete collapse of the Twin Towers and significant damage to the Pentagon. The events of 9/11 had profound implications, leading to the declaration of a global War on Terror by the United States, increased security measures worldwide, and significant shifts in geopolitics and international relations.[189]

In response to the question about the impact of the attack on U.S.-Israel relations, former Prime Minister Benjamin Netanyahu initially stated, "It's very good. Well, not very good, but it will generate immediate sympathy. [It will] strengthen the bond between our two peoples, because we've experienced terror over so many decades, but the United States has now experienced a massive haemorrhaging of terror."[190]

Prime Minister Ariel Sharon echoed this sentiment, affirming that the assault targeted "our common values" and "The fight against terrorism is an international struggle of the free world against the forces of darkness who seek to destroy our liberty and way of life."[191]

General Wesley Clark's Revelation: The Unveiling of Geopolitical Strategy (Nov 2001)

General Wesley Clark, a retired 4-star U.S. Army General and former Supreme Allied Commander of NATO (1997-2000), recounted his experience shortly after the events of 9/11. Approximately ten days after 9/11, he visited the Pentagon where he encountered Secretary Rumsfeld and Deputy Secretary Wolfowitz. While intending to greet former colleagues on the Joint Staff, a general summoned him for a conversation. The general informed him that a decision had been made to initiate war with Iraq, around September 20th. Perplexed, General Clark questioned the rationale behind this decision, to which the general admitted uncertainty, suggesting it was a response to the perceived lack of alternative actions in combating terrorism. Reflecting on the military's capacity to dismantle governments, the general expressed a sentiment likening it to viewing every problem as a nail when the only tool available is a hammer.[192]

Returning for a follow-up conversation weeks later, amid the ongoing military operations in Afghanistan, General Clark sought clarification on the status of plans regarding Iraq. However, he received startling information: a memo outlining a broader strategy to target seven countries within five years, starting with Iraq, and followed by Syria, Lebanon, Libya, Somalia, Sudan, and ending with Iran. This memo, deemed classified, was shared by the general, indicating the scope of geopolitical intentions within certain circles of authority.[193]

Benjamin Netanyahu's Testimony (2002)

Israeli Prime Minister Benjamin Netanyahu delivered a testimony on 12 Sep 2002 before the US House Government Reform Committee on the looming threat of Saddam Hussein's regime and the broader war against terror.[194]

Netanyahu: Did Israel launch that pre-emptive strike because Saddam had committed a specific act of terror against them? Did we coordinate our actions with the international community? Did we condition this operation on the approval of the United Nations? No, of course not. Israel acted because it understood, as we understood, that a nuclear-armed Saddam would place our very survival at risk.

And today, the United States must destroy the same regime because a nuclear-armed Saddam will place the security of our entire world at risk. Make no mistake about it: if and when Saddam has nuclear weapons, the terror network will have nuclear weapons. Once the terror network has nuclear weapons, it is only a matter of time before those weapons will be used. You cannot prevent a dictator who has used terrorism in the past, who supports and encourages terror organizations, from using this weapon or giving it to someone who will.

Once one of the principal regimes in the terror network has nuclear weapons, you cannot prevent the terror network from having nuclear weapons. Two decades ago, it was possible to thwart Saddam's nuclear ambitions by bombing a single installation. But today, nothing less than dismantling his regime will suffice because Saddam's nuclear program has fundamentally changed over those two decades. He no longer needs one large reactor to produce the deadly material necessary for atomic bombs. He can produce it in centrifuges the size of washing machines that can be hidden throughout the country.

I want to remind you that Iraq is a very big country. It is not the size of Monte Carlo; it is a large country. I believe that even free and unfettered inspections will not uncover these portable manufacturing sites of mass death. Knowing this, I ask all the governments and others who oppose or question the president's plan to look at it from the other end of the logic.

Representative: Do you believe that action can only be taken against Saddam after he builds nuclear bombs and uses them? And do various critics, especially overseas, believe that a clear connection between Saddam and September 11 must be established before we have the right to prevent the next September 11?

Netanyahu: Well, I think not. I'll try to give an analogy. All analogies are imperfect, but here's one: If you try to defeat the mafia, you don't just go after the foot soldiers who carried out the last attack or even stop with the apprehension of the particular don who sent them. You go after the entire network of organized crime—all the families, all the organizations. Likewise, if you intend to defeat terror, you don't just go after the terrorists who carried out the last attack or even the particular regime that sent them. You go after the entire network of terror—all the regimes that support terror, all the organizations they harbour. And doing this always entails the need to act before additional attacks are carried out. When the security of a nation is endangered, a responsible government has to take the necessary actions to protect its citizens and eliminate the threat that confronts them. Sometimes, this requires pre-emption. In the history of democracies, pre-emption has been, in my mind, the most difficult choice for leaders to make because, at the time of the decision, you can never prove the critics wrong; you can never show them the great catastrophe that was avoided by pre-emptive action. Yet, we now know that had the democracies taken pre-emptive action to bring down Hitler in the 1930s, the worst horrors in history could have been avoided.

Netanyahu: If you take out Saddam's regime, I guarantee you that it will have enormous positive reverberations in the region. People sitting right next door in Iran, young people, and many others will say the time of such regimes is gone, there is a new age, something new is happening.

Representative: Speculation on your part, or do you have some evidence to that effect?

Netanyahu: I was asked the same question in 1986. I had written a book in which I said that the way to deal with terrorist regimes was to apply military force against them, as we did in Afghanistan.

Representative: I haven't seen that sort of neighbourhood effect.

Netanyahu: But I think there's been an enormous effect. We were told that there would be tens of thousands of people streaming into Afghanistan, zealots who would be outraged by America's action, and this would produce a counter-reaction in the Arab world. But when you take an action like we did in Afghanistan, we're not going to see all the other countries just fold. What we saw is something else. First, we saw everybody streaming out of Afghanistan. The second thing we saw is all the Arab countries and many Muslim countries trying to side with America, trying to be okay with America.

The application of power is the most important thing in winning the war on terrorism. If I had to say what are the three principles of winning the war on terror, it's like the three principles of real estate: location, location, location. The three principles of winning the war on terror are the three W's: winning, winning, and winning. The more victories you amass, the easier the next victory becomes. The first victory in Afghanistan makes a second victory in Iraq that much easier. The second victory in Iraq will make the third victory that much easier too, but it may change the nature of achieving that victory.

Osama bin Laden's Anti-Israel Stance (2002)

Osama bin Laden, born in Saudi Arabia, rose to prominence during the Soviet-Afghan War in the 1980s, receiving support from the United States and other Western countries in their fight against the Soviet Union. However, his relationship with the U.S. soured over time as he formed Al-Qaeda, driven by anti-Western sentiments and opposition to Western influence in Muslim-majority nations. In 1998, bin Laden issued a fatwa declaring jihad against the United States and its allies, including Israel, citing reasons such as American military presence in Saudi Arabia and support for Israel. Throughout the 2000s, bin Laden criticized Israeli military actions against Palestinians, integrating anti-Israel sentiments into Al-Qaeda's ideology. On September 11, 2001, Al-Qaeda carried out a series of coordinated terrorist attacks against the United States.[195]

The "Letter to the American People," published on 24 Nov 2002, further emphasized bin Laden's anti-Israel stance, positioning the Israeli-Palestinian conflict within Al-Qaeda's broader mission against Western hegemony.[196]

"In the Name of God, the Most Gracious, the Most Merciful, Some American writers have published articles under the title 'On what basis are we fighting?'... Here we wanted to outline the truth - as an explanation and warning - hoping for Allah's reward, seeking success and support from Him. While seeking Allah's help, we form our reply based on two questions directed at the Americans: (Q1) Why are we fighting and opposing you? (Q2) What are we calling you to, and what do we want from you? Why are we fighting and opposing you? The answer is very simple: Because you attacked us and continue to attack us.

i. Palestine, which has sunk under military occupation for more than 80 years. The British handed over Palestine, with your help and support, to the Jews, who have occupied it for more than 50 years; years overflowing with oppression, tyranny, crimes, killing, expulsion, destruction, and devastation. The creation and continuation of Israel is one of the greatest crimes, and you are the leaders of its criminals. And of course, there is no need to explain and prove the degree of American support for Israel. The creation of Israel is a crime that must be erased. Each and every person whose hands have become polluted in the contribution towards this crime must pay its price, and pay for it heavily.

ii. It brings us both laughter and tears to see that you have not yet tired of repeating your fabricated lies that the Jews have a historical right to Palestine, as it was promised to them in the Torah. Anyone who disputes with them on this alleged fact is accused of antisemitism. This is one of the most fallacious, widely circulated fabrications in history. The people of Palestine are pure Arabs and original Semites. It is the Muslims who are the inheritors of Moses (peace be upon him) and the inheritors of the real Torah that has not been changed. Muslims believe in all of the Prophets, including Abraham, Moses, Jesus, and Muhammad, peace and blessings of Allah be upon them all. If the followers of Moses have been promised a right to Palestine in the Torah, then the Muslims are the most worthy nation of this. When the Muslims conquered Palestine and drove out the Romans, Palestine and Jerusalem returned to Islaam, the religion of all the Prophets peace be upon them. Therefore, the call to a historical right to Palestine cannot be raised against the Islamic Ummah that believes in all the Prophets of Allah (peace and blessings be upon them) - and we make no distinction between them.

iii. The blood pouring out of Palestine must be equally revenged. You must know that the Palestinians do not cry alone; their women are not widowed alone; their sons are not orphaned alone."...

The American people are the ones who choose their government by way of their own free will... Thus, the American people have chosen, consented to, and affirmed their support for the Israeli oppression of the Palestinians....

U.S. – led invasion of Iraq (2003)

In October 2002, the United States Congress passed a joint resolution that granted President George W. Bush the power to use military force against the Iraqi government. The Iraq War officially began on March 20, 2003, when the U.S., joined by the United Kingdom, Australia, and Poland, launched a "shock and awe" bombing campaign. Shortly following the bombing campaign, U.S.-led forces launched a ground invasion of Iraq. Iraqi forces were quickly overwhelmed as coalition forces swept through the country. The invasion led to the collapse of the Ba'athist government; Saddam Hussein was captured during Operation Red Dawn in December of that same year and executed three years later. [197]

The invasion of Iraq in 2003 was one of the most controversial military interventions in recent history. The primary justifications provided by the U.S. administration were the presence of weapons of mass destruction (WMDs) and alleged ties between Saddam Hussein's regime and terrorist organizations, particularly Al-Qaeda. However, following the invasion and subsequent occupation, no significant stockpiles of WMDs were found, which undermined the credibility of the initial rationale for the war. This absence raised questions about the intelligence used to justify the invasion and led to accusations of misinformation or manipulation by the U.S. government. [198]

Moreover, the post-invasion period was characterized by significant challenges, including widespread sectarian violence between Sunni and Shia communities, an insurgency against the U.S.-led coalition forces, and political instability. [199]

Israel's disengagement from Gaza Strip (2005)

Israel, despite facing significant political opposition domestically and enduring terrorist attacks during the Second Intifada, made the strategic decision to withdraw from the Gaza Strip in 2005. This withdrawal involved dismantling Israeli settlements and military installations with the aim of advancing the prospects for peace in the region. [200]

Despite the evacuation, the Gaza Strip remained a contentious area, with ongoing debates about its legal status and control. The aftermath of the disengagement saw Hamas gaining control of the Gaza Strip. [201]

Second Lebanon War (2006)

The 2006 Lebanon War, also known as the Israel–Hezbollah War and the Second Lebanon War, was a 34-day military conflict in Lebanon, northern Israel, and the Golan Heights. The primary parties involved were Hezbollah paramilitary forces and the Israel Defense Forces (IDF). The conflict began on July 12, 2006, and lasted until a United Nations-brokered ceasefire took effect on August 14, 2006, although it formally ended on September 8, 2006, when Israel lifted its naval blockade of Lebanon. [202]

The conflict was triggered by a Hezbollah cross-border raid, during which Hezbollah fighters attacked Israeli border towns and captured two Israeli soldiers. This event prompted airstrikes and artillery barrages from Israel, targeting Lebanon, including civilian infrastructure. In retaliation, Hezbollah launched rockets into northern Israel and engaged in guerrilla warfare against the IDF. The conflict inflicted significant casualties, with approximately 1,191 to 1,300 Lebanese individuals and 165 Israelis killed and caused extensive damage to infrastructure in both Lebanon and Israel. [203]

Resolution 1701, passed on August 11, 2006, by the United Nations Security Council, called for Hezbollah's disarmament, the IDF's withdrawal from Lebanon, and the deployment of Lebanese Armed Forces and an expanded UNIFIL presence. However, Hezbollah remains armed, and there is reluctance from the Lebanese government and UNIFIL to enforce disarmament. The war ended in a 2008 prisoner exchange, with Hezbollah claiming victory and Israel seeing it as a failure. [204]

Hamas's victory in the Palestinian legislative election (2006)

In 2006, Hamas won the Palestinian legislative election by campaigning on clean government without corruption, combined with affirmation of Palestinians' right to struggle against the Israeli occupation, thus winning a majority in the Palestinian Legislative Council.[205] In 2007, Hamas took control of the Gaza Strip from the rival Palestinian faction Fatah, which it has governed separately from the Palestinian National Authority. This takeover was followed by an Israeli blockade of the Gaza Strip with Egyptian support. The blockade severely restricted the movement of goods and people in and out of Gaza, exacerbating humanitarian conditions in the region. [206]

The Israel Lobby: John Mearsheimer and Stephen Walt (2006)

"The Israel Lobby and U.S. Foreign Policy," authored by John Mearsheimer and Stephen Walt, is a controversial academic paper published in 2006. John Joseph Mearsheimer is a distinguished American political scientist and international relations scholar, currently holding the position of the R. Wendell Harrison Distinguished Service Professor at the University of Chicago. He is renowned for his contributions to the realist school of thought. Mearsheimer gained prominence for his development of offensive realism, a theory that posits the behaviour of great powers in the international system is primarily motivated by the rational pursuit of regional hegemony within an anarchic global framework. He argues that states seek to maximize their power and security, often leading to competition and conflict. [207]

Throughout his career, John Mearsheimer has made significant contributions to security studies, nuclear proliferation, and U.S. foreign policy. He is known for his realist perspectives on international issues, including his critical examination of U.S. foreign policy, the Israel-Palestine conflict, and the role of great powers in global affairs. Mearsheimer has also delved into contemporary topics such as U.S.-China relations and the Russia-Ukraine war. He is noted for his predictions regarding the conflict in Ukraine. In a 2014 article titled "Why the Ukraine Crisis Is the West's Fault," published in Foreign Affairs, Mearsheimer argued that the West's efforts to integrate Ukraine into Western institutions such as NATO and the EU provoked a hostile reaction from Russia. He suggested that these actions would lead to increased tensions and potential conflict between Russia and Ukraine. [208]

In their 2007 book, which followed their influential paper "The Israel Lobby and U.S. Foreign Policy," Mearsheimer and Walt assert the existence of a powerful "Israel Lobby" in the United States. This lobby, they argue, consists of pro-Israel interest groups like AIPAC (American Israel Public Affairs Committee), individuals, and organizations, and exerts considerable influence over U.S. foreign policy in the Middle East. According to Mearsheimer and Walt, this influence often results in U.S. policies that prioritize Israel's interests over broader American objectives. Their work sparked extensive debate and criticism, with some praising its analysis while others accused the authors of anti-Semitism or bias. [209]

Operation Outside the Box, Syria (2007)

In 2007, the discovery of the Al Kibar nuclear reactor in Syria, resembling North Korea's Yongbyon facility, raised significant concerns for Israel and the U.S., particularly regarding North Korea's suspected involvement. Israeli Prime Minister Ehud Olmert stressed the importance of preventing Syria from acquiring nuclear weapons, invoking the Begin Doctrine. Operation Outside the Box, also known as Operation Orchard, was an Israeli airstrike on the suspected nuclear reactor site in the Deir ez-Zor region of Syria, occurring just after midnight on September 6, 2007. [210]

Unlike previous strikes, such as the one against Iraq, the airstrike against Syria did not provoke international outcry, partly due to Israel's silence regarding the attack and Syria's efforts to cover up its activities. The raid, officially confirmed by the Israeli government in 2018, involved Israeli Air Force (IAF) F-15Is and F-16Is equipped with Maverick missiles and bombs. Elite Israeli special forces commandos may have also been involved, using sophisticated electronic warfare capabilities to neutralize Syria's air defense systems during the operation. [211]

Annapolis Conference (2007)

The Annapolis Conference, held in November 2007, was a significant international gathering aimed at restarting Israeli-Palestinian peace negotiations. It took place at the United States Naval Academy in Annapolis, Maryland, and was hosted by then-US President George W. Bush. The conference brought together key stakeholders, including Israeli Prime Minister Ehud Olmert and Palestinian President Mahmoud Abbas, as well as representatives from various Arab states and other nations. [212]

The primary goal of the Annapolis Conference was to relaunch negotiations towards a two-state solution to the Israeli-Palestinian conflict, with the establishment of an independent Palestinian state alongside Israel. The conference culminated in a joint statement by Israeli and Palestinian leaders, reaffirming their commitment to reaching a final peace agreement. While the Annapolis Conference generated some optimism and momentum for renewed peace talks, the negotiations that followed faced numerous challenges and setbacks, and a final agreement was not reached. However, the conference remains noteworthy as a diplomatic effort to address one of the most entrenched conflicts in the Middle East. [213]

Operation Cast Lead (2008-2009)

Operation Cast Lead, also known as the Gaza War, was a military offensive conducted by the Israel Defense Forces (IDF) against the Gaza Strip from December 27, 2008, to January 18, 2009. The operation aimed to stop rocket attacks from Gaza into Israeli territory and to weaken Hamas, which had controlled Gaza since 2007. [214]

The offensive resulted in significant casualties and damage on both sides. Palestinian sources estimated that over 1,400 Palestinians, including civilians, militants, and children, were killed, and thousands more were injured. Israel reported 13 deaths, including three civilians and ten soldiers. The operation also caused widespread destruction of infrastructure and homes in Gaza. [215] Operation Cast Lead sparked widespread condemnation and criticism from the international community, particularly regarding civilian casualties and the disproportionate use of force by Israel. The United Nations and human rights organizations raised concerns about violations of international humanitarian law and called for independent investigations into alleged war crimes. [216]

The offensive ended with a ceasefire brokered by Egypt on January 18, 2009. Under the terms of the ceasefire, both Israel and Hamas agreed to halt hostilities, and Israel committed to easing its blockade of Gaza. However, the ceasefire was fragile and did not address the underlying issues of the Israeli-Palestinian conflict. [217]

The Invention of the Jewish People (2009)

Shlomo Sand is an Israeli Emeritus Professor of History at Tel Aviv University, known for his controversial perspectives on Jewish history and the state of Israel. Born in Linz, Austria, to Polish Jewish Holocaust survivors, Sand spent his early years in a displaced persons camp near Munich. He earned a BA in History from Tel Aviv University in 1975 before moving to France. In Paris, he studied and taught, obtaining an MA in French History and a PhD for his thesis on Georges Sorel and Marxism. Since 1982, Sand has taught at Tel Aviv University, as well as at the University of California, Berkeley, and the École des hautes études en sciences sociales in Paris. [218]

"The Invention of the Land of Israel" by Shlomo Sand is a book that challenges the notion of a shared Jewish identity and the invented history of the "Land of Israel." Sand argues that Jews have no common ethnic lineage due to high levels of conversion in antiquity and no common language beyond prayer. He further questions what unites Jews, asserting that religion and Zionism are political constructs. He highlights that traditional Judaism lacked a strong emphasis on returning to this land and suggests that Christian Zionists played a significant role in popularizing this idea in the 19th century. The term "Land of Israel" is scarcely mentioned in the Old Testament, with the more common expression being the Land of Canaan. Biblical "Israel" refers only to northern Israel (Samaria).

Sand argues that the creation of the "State of Israel" was not due to God's promise of a return to a long-lost land but rather to the Holocaust and the reluctance of the West to provide a refuge for its survivors. Sand's work debunks a nationalist mythology that holds sway in large sections of popular opinion and normalizes Jews by challenging exceptionalist beliefs. While the Holocaust was a unique event, the nationalist narrative is similar across nations, forming a literary genre that balances self-pitying victimhood and vainglorious heroic deeds. [219]

Sand's book has generated heated controversy and has been translated into several languages. It has been praised by some historians for normalizing Jewish history and dismantling nationalist historical myths, while others have criticized it for being baseless and incoherent, particularly in its claims about Zionist and contemporary Israeli historiography. The book has also been debated for its thesis that the majority of modern Eastern European Jewry originated from the Khazar kingdom, a claim that has been widely debated and rejected. [220] Shlomo Sand's views on Israel and the Jewish people have been controversial, and he has faced criticism from both Israeli and international scholars. However, he remains a prominent and influential figure in Israeli academia, and his work continues to be widely discussed and debated.

Settlement Freeze (2009-2010)

A significant development in the Israeli-Palestinian conflict was the implementation of a settlement freeze in 2009-2010 by Israeli Prime Minister Benjamin Netanyahu. This move came in response to efforts by U.S. President Barack Obama to revive peace talks between Israel and the Palestinians, following Obama's inauguration earlier in 2009. President Obama's administration emphasized the importance of achieving a two-state solution to the Israeli-Palestinian conflict, with Obama reaffirming this commitment in a speech at Cairo University. The settlement freeze was seen as a goodwill gesture toward the Palestinians and a step toward restarting negotiations. [221]

The freeze, lasting for 10 months, halted Israeli construction in West Bank settlements, a key demand of the Palestinian Authority led by President Mahmoud Abbas. While the freeze led to a brief resumption of peace talks between Israeli and Palestinian negotiators, ultimately, the talks did not progress significantly, and President Abbas decided to halt the negotiations. [222]

Assassination of Hamas Commander Mahmoud Al-Mabhouh in Dubai (2010)

In January 2010, Mahmoud Al-Mabhouh, a senior Hamas military commander, was assassinated in Dubai, United Arab Emirates, under suspicious circumstances. CCTV footage and other evidence suggested the involvement of at least 26 agents traveling on forged passports. While the UAE police and Hamas accused Israel and Mossad of the assassination, no direct evidence linking Mossad to the crime was found. The use of fake passports, including British, Irish, and Australian documents, raised international concerns. Emirati authorities claimed to have fingerprint and DNA evidence implicating the attackers, leading Dubai's police chief to openly accuse Mossad of the murder. [223]

Arab Spring (2010)

The Arab Spring was a series of pro-democracy uprisings that swept across the Arab world starting in late 2010. These uprisings were largely driven by frustrations with authoritarian regimes, political repression, economic inequality, and lack of opportunities. The protests were facilitated by social media and communication technologies, allowing for the rapid spread of information and organization of demonstrations. [224]

The Arab Spring began in Tunisia in December 2010, sparked by the self-immolation of Mohamed Bouazizi, a street vendor who was protesting police corruption and harassment. The Tunisian protests quickly escalated into a nationwide movement demanding the ouster of President Zine El Abidine Ben Ali, who fled the country in January 2011. The success of the Tunisian revolution inspired similar movements in other Arab countries, such as Egypt, Libya, Yemen, Syria, and Bahrain. [225]

Uprising in Egypt (2011)

The Arab Spring uprising in Egypt, which began in early 2011, marked a significant turning point in the country's modern history. Fuelled by frustration with the autocratic rule of President Hosni Mubarak and widespread socio-economic grievances, Egyptians took to the streets in mass protests demanding political reform, social justice, and an end to corruption. The protests, largely organized through social media platforms, gained momentum rapidly and culminated in the iconic eighteen-day uprising cantered in Cairo's Tahrir Square. Millions of Egyptians from diverse backgrounds and ideologies united in a call for change, capturing the world's attention and inspiring similar movements across the Arab world. [226]

On February 11, 2011, Mubarak, who had ruled Egypt for nearly three decades, stepped down, handing power to the military and sparking hope for a new era of democracy and freedom. Mubarak had maintained a stable peace treaty with Israel since 1979. Subsequently, the Supreme Council of the Armed Forces (SCAF) assumed control of the country's affairs, promising a transition to civilian rule and democratic elections. [227]

However, the euphoria of Mubarak's ousting soon gave way to uncertainty and political turbulence. The transition period witnessed a power struggle between various political factions, including secularists, Islamists, and remnants of the old regime. Tensions flared over the drafting of a new constitution, the role of the military, and the trajectory of Egypt's democratic transition. In the first post-revolution presidential elections held in 2012, Mohamed Morsi, a member of the Muslim Brotherhood's Freedom and Justice Party, emerged victorious, becoming Egypt's first democratically elected president. The rise of the Muslim Brotherhood and subsequent political instability in Egypt raised concerns in Israel about the future of the peace agreement. [228]

Morsi's presidency was marked by deep political divisions within Egypt, with clashes between his Islamist supporters, mainly the Muslim Brotherhood, and various opposition groups. Critics accused Morsi of authoritarian practices and consolidating power within the Muslim Brotherhood, further alienating segments of the population. Mass protests erupted in June 2013, fuelled by grievances over governance failures and fears of increasing Islamist influence. [229] In July 2013, amid mass protests against his rule, Morsi was ousted in a military coup led by then-Defense

Minister Abdel Fatah al-Sisi. Al-Sisi, who later became president, launched a severe crackdown on political dissent, stifling opposition voices and rolling back many of the gains of the revolution. [230]

Turkish Prime Minister Recep Tayyip Erdogan claimed that Israel was behind the military coup in Egypt that ousted President Mohamed Morsi. A CIA document from the Freedom of Information Act Electronic Reading Room suggests that Erdogan mentioned a meeting between Turkey's justice minister and an unnamed "Jewish" intellectual in France before Egypt's 2011 elections. The intellectual purportedly stated that "democracy is not the ballot box," implying that even if the Muslim Brotherhood were to win the elections, they would not be allowed to remain in power. However, Erdogan did not clarify the intellectual's connection to the Israeli government or how their opinion influenced Israel's involvement in the ouster of President Mohamed Morsi in Egypt. [231]

A top-secret cable leaked to Al Jazeera revealed that Mossad, Israel's foreign intelligence service, sought detailed information from its South African counterparts on Egypt's first democratically elected president, Mohamed Morsi, and key figures in his Muslim Brotherhood movement. Dated July 30, 2012, the cable raises questions about Mossad's intentions and the broader implications of its inquiries. Morsi's subsequent ousting in a military coup in June 2013 highlights the significance of this. The term "Deep State," used in the cable, alludes to entrenched power structures within Egypt that played a pivotal role in Morsi's downfall and paved the way for General Abdel Fatah al-Sisi's rise to power. Al-Sisi's presidency, marked by warm relations with Israel, underscores the depth of cooperation between the two nations.[232]

The Syrian Civil War (2011)

The Syrian Civil War, sparked by discontent with the Assad regime during the Arab Spring protests, evolved into a multifaceted conflict involving various domestic and international actors.[233]

Bashar al-Assad's government has been a central actor in the conflict. Assad, who succeeded his father Hafez al-Assad as president in 2000, has sought to maintain power and control over Syria. The regime has used military force against rebel-held areas and civilian populations. Assad has received support from Russia, Iran, and Hezbollah in Lebanon.

Russia has been a key ally of the Assad regime since the beginning of the conflict. In 2015, Russia intervened militarily in Syria, launching airstrikes against opposition forces and Islamic extremist groups. Russian support has been crucial in bolstering Assad's position and regaining territory lost to rebel groups. Russia's involvement has also been motivated by strategic interests in the Middle East, including maintaining access to its naval base in Tartus and countering Western influence in the region.

Iran has provided extensive military and financial support to the Assad regime throughout the conflict. Iranian forces, including the Islamic Revolutionary Guard Corps (IRGC), as well as proxy militias, such as Hezbollah from Lebanon, have been deployed to Syria to fight alongside government forces. Iran sees Syria as a key ally and a crucial link in its regional influence.

The opposition to Assad's regime has been fragmented, consisting of various rebel groups with differing ideologies and goals. These groups include secular Free Syrian Army (FSA) factions, Islamist groups like Ahrar al-Sham and Jaysh al-Islam, and jihadist organizations such as Hayat Tahrir al-Sham (formerly known as Jabhat al-Nusra, an al-Qaeda affiliate), and the Islamic State of Iraq and the Levant (ISIL/ISIS). Over time, infighting and competition among rebel groups, as well as the rise of extremist factions, have weakened the opposition.

Turkey has been involved in the conflict, primarily in support of rebel factions fighting against the Assad regime. Turkey has provided military aid to certain rebel groups, facilitated the movement of fighters and supplies across its border with Syria, and launched military operations against Kurdish forces in northern Syria, whom it views as a threat due to their links to the Kurdistan Workers' Party (PKK).

The United States and its Western allies initially supported moderate rebel factions and called for Assad's removal from power. However, their involvement has been limited compared to regional actors like Russia, Iran, and Turkey. The U.S. has conducted airstrikes against ISIS targets in Syria and provided support to Kurdish-led Syrian Democratic Forces (SDF) in the fight against ISIS. The Trump administration also launched airstrikes against Syrian government targets in response to the use of chemical weapons

Kurdish-led forces, particularly the People's Protection Units (YPG) and its political counterpart, the Democratic Union Party (PYD), have played a significant role in the conflict, especially in northern Syria. The Kurdish-led Syrian Democratic Forces (SDF) have been a key ally of the U.S. in the fight against ISIS. However, Turkey considers the YPG/PYD to be terrorist organizations due to their links to the PKK and has launched military operations against them in northern Syria.

These are some of the main parties involved in the Syrian Civil War, each with its own interests, alliances, and objectives, contributing to the complexity and protracted nature of the conflict.[234]

Assad regime has managed to regain control over much of the country with the help of its allies, significant pockets of opposition and jihadist resistance persist. The humanitarian crisis continues unabated, with millions of Syrians displaced and in need of urgent assistance. The conflict has also fuelled instability in the wider region, exacerbating tensions and threatening the security of neighbouring countries. Despite numerous attempts at diplomacy and ceasefires, a lasting political solution remains elusive, leaving the Syrian people to endure ongoing suffering and uncertainty.[235]

Palestinian UN Membership Bid (2011)

In 2011, Mahmoud Abbas, representing the Palestinian Authority, submitted an application for Palestinian membership to the United Nations, aiming to become the 194th member. This bid failed due to insufficient support from nine out of the 15 Security Council members, with the United States vetoing the resolution supporting Palestinian membership. [236] However, in November 2012, the Palestinian Authority successfully obtained non-member observer state status with the backing of over two-thirds of General Assembly members. This elevation in status within the U.N. system enabled them to join various international organizations, including the International Criminal Court. Despite this advancement, achieving full independence still depends on negotiating a peace agreement with Israel. [237]

Operation Pillar of Defence (2012)

Operation Pillar of Defence was a military campaign conducted by Israel in Gaza in November 2012. The operation aimed to curb rocket attacks from the Gaza Strip into Israeli territory, particularly by targeting militant leaders and infrastructure associated with Hamas. The escalation reached a critical point on November 14, 2012, when the Israel Defense Forces (IDF) carried out a targeted airstrike that killed Ahmed Jabari, the commander of Hamas's military wing, the Izz ad-Din al-Qassam Brigades.[238]

The conflict lasted for eight days and resulted in casualties on both sides. A ceasefire brokered by Egypt ended the hostilities, highlighting ongoing security challenges and complexities in the Israeli-Palestinian conflict. The conflict reaffirmed the threat that Hamas posed to Israel, especially after the much larger 2009 conflict. Hamas' firing of rockets into Israeli civilian areas led to increased investment in Israel's Iron Dome missile defense system, as well as bomb shelters and a civilian alert system. Additionally, the conflict renewed international criticism of Israeli policies, including questions over the use of disproportionate force by human rights groups.[239]

Operation Protective Edge (2014)

Operation Protective Edge was a military operation conducted by Israel in the summer of 2014. It was launched in response to escalating rocket attacks from Gaza into Israeli territory by Hamas. The operation aimed to stop the rocket fire and destroy Hamas' infrastructure, including its network of tunnels used for smuggling weapons and launching attacks.[240]

The conflict resulted in significant casualties and destruction on both sides. Israel faced criticism for the high number of civilian casualties in Gaza, while Hamas was condemned for firing rockets indiscriminately into civilian areas in Israel. During the conflict, over

2,000 people were killed in Gaza, mainly Gazan Palestinians, while 69 Israelis also lost their lives. The operation lasted for about seven weeks before a ceasefire was reached, mediated by Egypt, on August 26, 2014. However, the underlying issues and tensions between Israel and Hamas remained unresolved, leading to periodic flare-ups of violence in the years since.[241]

Netanyahu's Assertion that Palestinian Inspired Holocaust (2015)

In 2015, Benjamin Netanyahu, then the Prime Minister of Israel, made a contentious statement suggesting that a Palestinian religious leader, Haj Amin al-Husseini, influenced Adolf Hitler to annihilate the Jews during the Holocaust. This remark, delivered during a speech at the World Zionist Congress in Jerusalem, ignited significant backlash from politicians, historians, and the public both within Israel and globally.[242]

This statement was widely condemned as a dangerous historical distortion that trivializes the Holocaust. Historians, including those from Yad Vashem (Israel's official memorial to the victims of the Holocaust) and Tel Aviv University, rejected Netanyahu's assertion, stating that the historical record does not support the idea that al-Husseini was the one who gave Hitler the idea for the final solution. They emphasized that the meeting between Hitler and al-Husseini occurred after the Nazis had already begun implementing the extermination of Jews.[243]

Opposition leaders in Israel, such as Isaac Herzog and Itzik Shmuli, strongly criticized Netanyahu's statement, calling it a "dangerous historical distortion" that plays into the hands of Holocaust deniers. They demanded that Netanyahu correct his remarks immediately.[244]

Saeb Erekat, secretary-general of the Palestine Liberation Organization (PLO), highlighted the role Palestinians played in fighting the Nazis during the Second World War. "Palestine will never forget, although it seems Netanyahu's extremist government has. It is a sad day in history when the leader of the Israeli government hates his neighbour so much that he is willing to absolve the most notorious war criminal in history, Adolf Hitler, of the murder of six million Jews," Despite initial attempts to clarify his remarks, Netanyahu ultimately retracted the accusation against al-Husseini after facing extensive local and international condemnation for distorting historical facts.[245]

Netanyahu on Iran Nuclear Deal at UN (2015)

The Iran nuclear deal, formally known as the Joint Comprehensive Plan of Action (JCPOA), was a landmark agreement reached on July 14, 2015, in Vienna, Austria, between Iran and five permanent members of the UN Security Council (China, France, Russia, the United Kingdom, and the United States) and Germany—collectively known as the P5+1 to address concerns about Iran's nuclear program.[246]

Israeli Prime Minister Benjamin Netanyahu delivered a scathing condemnation of this nuclear deal in his address to the U.N. General Assembly in New York on 01 Oct 2015. Netanyahu described the agreement as a "historic mistake" and emphasized that it would not prevent Iran from acquiring nuclear weapons. He argued that the deal's limitations on Iran's nuclear program allowing Iran to pursue its nuclear ambitions without any significant constraints. Netanyahu also highlighted the financial benefits Iran would gain from the deal, stating that the lifting of sanctions would provide the country with hundreds of billions of dollars to fund its global terrorism and regional aggression. He warned that this financial windfall would fuel Iran's efforts to eliminate Israel, which he described as a grave threat to the Jewish state's existence.[247]

Netanyahu's speech was part of a broader Israeli campaign against the deal, which had been met with significant criticism from the Israeli government and many of its allies. The deal was seen as a compromise that would allow Iran to maintain a nuclear program while providing relief from economic sanctions. Netanyahu and other Israeli leaders argued that this compromise would ultimately lead to a nuclear-armed Iran, which would pose a significant threat to regional stability and Israel's security.[248]

Assassination of Hamas Engineer Mohamed Zouari (2016)

Mohamed Zouari, also known as "The Engineer," was a Tunisian aerospace engineer and member of Hamas' military wing. His assassination in 2016 sent shockwaves through the region. Fleeing political repression in Tunisia, Zouari moved to Syria in 1991, where he acquired knowledge in aeronautics and drone design. He then joined the Izz al-Din al-Qassam Brigades, overseeing the development of the Ababeel-1 unmanned aircraft, the first Palestinian reconnaissance UAV.[249]

After the Tunisian Revolution (2010-2011), Zouari returned to Tunisia. However, he was gunned down outside his home in Sfax, Tunisia, sparking accusations against Israel's Mossad intelligence agency. Tunisian authorities initiated an investigation, though progress was slow. Zouari's killing exacerbated tensions between Israel and Hamas, shedding light on the use of targeted assassinations in the Israeli-Palestinian conflict. The incident underscored the complexities of regional conflicts and the human cost of unresolved disputes.[250]

Hamas's 2017 Charter: A Comprehensive Overview

Hamas, the Palestinian militant group, released its new charter in 2017, marking a significant development in its ideological stance. The charter outlines Hamas's core principles, objectives, and its perspective on the Israeli-Palestinian conflict.[251]

The 2017 Charter is more pragmatic and less ideological, reflecting Hamas's evolving political strategy and its desire to broaden its appeal to Palestinians and the international community. One of the most significant changes in the 2017 Charter is the shift in Hamas's stance towards the Palestinian-Israeli conflict. While the 1988 Charter framed the conflict as a religious war between Muslims and Jews, the 2017 Charter defines it as a struggle against the "Zionist project" rather than Jews in general. This change reflects Hamas's recognition of the complexity of the conflict and its desire to appeal to a broader Palestinian and international audience.

Another significant change in the 2017 Charter is Hamas's acceptance of a Palestinian state within the armistice lines, also known as the 1967 borders. This is a significant departure from the 1988 Charter, which called for the establishment of an Islamic state in all of historic Palestine.

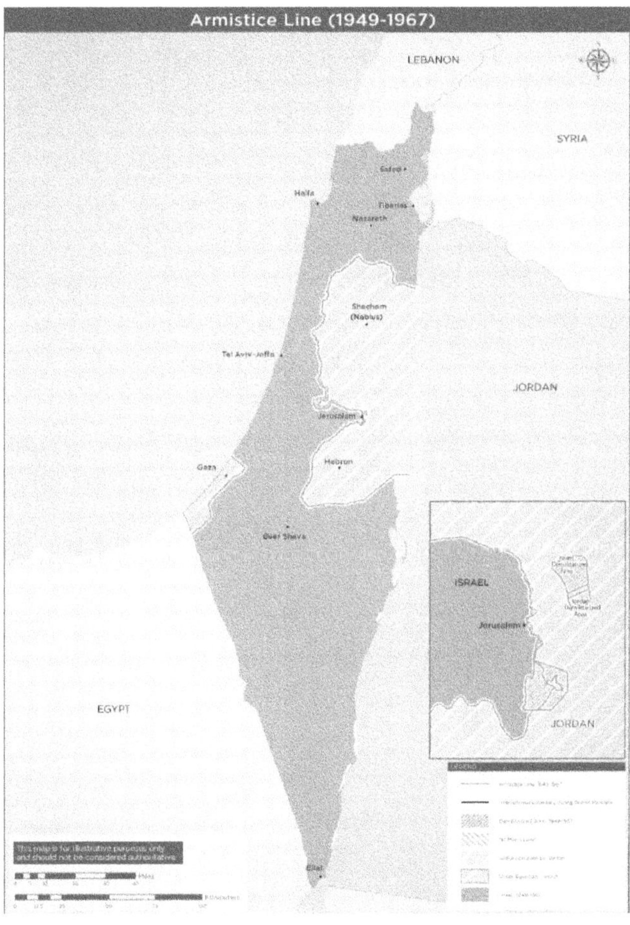

Figure 9. 1967 borders (BBC,2023)

The 2017 Charter also states that Hamas remains open to democratic political competition with Palestinian rivals, underscoring its commitment to democratic principles. However, the 2017 Charter also reaffirms Hamas's commitment to resistance and its opposition to normalization with Israel. Hamas views the Palestinian issue as the central cause for the Arab and Islamic Ummah and believes in cooperating with all states that support the rights of the Palestinian people.[252]

Trump Administration's Recognition of Jerusalem (2017)

In December 2017, President Donald Trump announced a significant shift in U.S. policy towards Israel by officially recognizing Jerusalem as the capital of Israel. This declaration departed from decades of U.S. policy, which had maintained that the status of Jerusalem should be determined through negotiations between Israelis and Palestinians as part of a broader peace agreement. This ignited widespread international condemnation, especially from Arab and Muslim nations, fearing increased tensions and hindrance to the Israeli-Palestinian peace process. Protests erupted globally, some escalating into violence. The UN General Assembly convened, with an overwhelming majority opposing the U.S. recognition.[253]

During his presidential campaign, Trump had addressed the AIPAC Policy Conference in March 2016. His speech aimed to reassure the pro-Israel audience of his commitment to the U.S.-Israel relationship, despite scepticism from some in the Jewish community about his candidacy. Trump's speech emphasized his support for Israel's security and his intention to move the U.S. embassy in Israel from Tel Aviv to Jerusalem, a promise that he later fulfilled as president. Trump's approach to the Middle East, particularly his administration's stance on issues like the Iran nuclear deal and the Israeli-Palestinian conflict, generally aligned with the positions advocated by AIPAC. Trump withdrew the United States from the Iran nuclear deal, a move strongly opposed by AIPAC, which viewed the agreement as insufficient in addressing Iran's nuclear ambitions and its support for terrorism.[254]

Trump's son-in-law and senior adviser, Jared Kushner, who played a key role in shaping Trump's Middle East policy, has close ties to Israel through his family's real estate business and personal connections. Jared Kushner, born January 10, 1981, in Livingston, New Jersey. His paternal grandparents were Holocaust survivors. Raised in a Modern Orthodox Jewish family, he attended the Frisch School and Harvard University, where his father's donation sparked controversy. He was a key architect of the "Peace to Prosperity" plan, which sought to address the conflict by focusing on economic development in the Palestinian territories. Additionally, Kushner was instrumental in brokering the Abraham Accords, which normalized diplomatic relations between Israel and several Arab states.[255]

Despite the controversy and criticism surrounding President Trump's decision, the U.S. embassy was officially relocated to Jerusalem in May 2018. The move was celebrated by Israeli officials but condemned by Palestinians and much of the international community, who viewed it as prejudicing the outcome of future negotiations on Jerusalem's status.[256]

Netanyahu's Policy towards Hamas (2019)

For years, successive governments led by Benjamin Netanyahu pursued a strategy that exacerbated the divide between the Gaza Strip and the West Bank, weakening the Palestinian Authority (PA) under Mahmoud Abbas while inadvertently empowering the Hamas organization. This policy, driven by the desire to hinder any progress towards Palestinian statehood, resulted in Hamas transitioning from a mere terrorist entity to a de facto governing body in Gaza. Israel engaged in indirect negotiations with Hamas through intermediaries like Egypt and Qatar, allowing cash infusions into Gaza and facilitating discussions on increasing work permits for

Gazan labourers. While these measures were intended to maintain a fragile calm, they ultimately bolstered Hamas's grip on power.[257]

In March 2019, Netanyahu himself admitted that he supported the policy of enriching Hamas to keep the PA at bay. "Whoever opposes a Palestinian state must support delivery of funds to Gaza because maintaining separation between the PA in the West Bank and Hamas in Gaza will prevent the establishment of a Palestinian state," he said during a meeting with Likud MKs (Members of Knesset).[258]

In May 2019, former Egyptian President Hosni Mubarak further confirmed this during an interview: "Netanyahu isn't interested in a two-state solution. Rather, he wants to separate Gaza from the West Bank, as he told me at the end of 2010."[259]

In August 2019, former Prime Minister Ehud Barak told Israeli Army Radio that Netanyahu's "strategy is to keep Hamas alive and kicking… even at the price of abandoning the citizens [of the south]… in order to weaken the Palestinian Authority in Ramallah."[260]

Recognition of Israeli Sovereignty over the Golan Heights (2019)

In March 2019, U.S. President Donald Trump signed a proclamation officially recognizing Israeli sovereignty over the Golan Heights, a territory Israel captured from Syria during the 1967 Six-Day War.[261] The majority of the international community criticized the move, asserting that it violated international law and impeded peace efforts in the Israeli-Palestinian conflict. Furthermore, several countries reiterated their dedication to UN Security Council Resolution 242, which mandates Israel's withdrawal from territories occupied in 1967, including the Golan Heights. Overall, the proclamation prompted a mixed global reaction, with some supporting the decision while many others condemned it.[262]

Peace to Prosperity plan (2020)

In January 2020, U.S. President Donald Trump unveiled the "Peace to Prosperity" plan, led by Jared Kushner, Trump's son-in-law and senior advisor. The plan presented a vision for a two-state solution but with specific parameters. It proposed Israeli sovereignty over certain settlements in the West Bank, as well as key regions like the Jordan Valley and Jerusalem. Additionally, it suggested the establishment of a demilitarized Palestinian state in parts of the West Bank and Gaza. The plan also included an economic component, unveiled at a conference in Bahrain in June 2019, which aimed to promote economic development in Palestinian territories. Moreover, it required recognition of Israel as a Jewish state and the renunciation of terrorism by Palestinians. Despite its intentions to offer a pathway to a two-state solution, the plan faced significant criticism from various quarters.[263]

Critics raised concerns about the plan's lack of Palestinian input, the Israeli annexation of the West Bank violating international law, the recognition of Jerusalem as Israel's capital disregarding Palestinian aspirations, the fragmented viability of the proposed Palestinian state, and the plan diverging from international consensus on key issues like borders and Jerusalem.[264]

Figure 10. Prosperity Plan (New York Times, 2020)

In February 2020, Mahmoud Abbas, the President of the Palestinian Authority, addressed the United Nations Security Council, describing the Trump administration's peace plan as "Swiss cheese," implying that it was full of holes or inconsistencies.[265]

The Abraham Accords (2020)

The Abraham Accords, signed in 2020, represent a historic milestone in Middle Eastern diplomacy, marking the normalization of relations between Israel and several Arab countries, including the United Arab Emirates (UAE), Bahrain, Morocco, and Sudan.[266] The Accords were based on a simple premise that diplomacy and communication would promote greater stability, prosperity, and hope in the region. In exchange for Morocco normalizing relations with Israel, the United States recognized Western Sahara as part of Morocco.[267] The Accords have led to new forms of cooperation in the Middle East and beyond, fostering diplomatic relations and cooperation, expanding trade and commerce, deepening people-to-people ties, and promoting a more integrated region.[268]

However, the Accords have also raised questions about the future of Palestinian aspirations for statehood and the prospects for a negotiated peace settlement. The Accords serve as a model for potential future agreements between Israel and other Arab and Muslim-majority countries, signalling a shift in regional dynamics and underscoring the importance of pragmatism, mutual interests, and external factors in shaping regional diplomacy.[269]

Assassination of Major General Qasem Soleimani (2020)

On January 3, 2020, Qasem Soleimani, an Iranian Major General, was assassinated by an American drone strike near Baghdad International Airport, Iraq. He was traveling to meet Iraqi Prime Minister Adil Abdul-Mahdi at the time. Soleimani was the commander of the Quds Force, one of the five branches of Iran's Islamic Revolutionary Guard Corps (IRGC). Soleimani held significant influence in Iran, being subordinate only to Supreme Leader Ali Khamenei. Alongside Soleimani, five Iraqi nationals and four other Iranian nationals were killed. The Pentagon stated that Soleimani and his troops were responsible for the deaths of hundreds of American and coalition service members.[270]

At his rally in Florida in October 2023, Donald Trump said he stands with Israel. At the same time, he criticized Netanyahu for letting him down in the past. Trump further said:

"Under my leadership, we will stand with Israel 100%. And we will not let them fail. However, I must recount a troubling experience we faced in our partnership with Israel, particularly in the pursuit of justice against Qasem Soleimani, a notorious threat to our security. It was a collaborative effort between the United States and Israel, meticulously planned for weeks and months. We knew every detail, from his whereabouts to his mode of operation. Yet, the night before our decisive action, a distressing development arose. Israel unexpectedly withdrew from the operation, leaving us questioning and concerned. Despite our shared goals and extensive preparation, they chose not to participate without explanation. It was a setback, a betrayal of trust that resonated deeply."[271]

11 Day War (2021)

In May 2021, a significant escalation of conflict occurred between Israel and Palestinian factions, primarily triggered by events in Jerusalem's Sheikh Jarrah neighbourhood. Tensions rose due to the threat of Palestinian evictions by Israeli settlers, leading to protests and clashes. The situation intensified during Ramadan, with clashes at the Al-Aqsa Mosque compound. Subsequently, Hamas and Islamic Jihad launched rocket attacks from Gaza into Israeli cities, prompting Israeli airstrikes in response.[272] The conflict resulted in civilian casualties and widespread destruction. At least 256 Palestinians, including 66 children, were killed, along with at least 13 Israelis, including two children. Diplomatic efforts, led by France, Egypt, and Jordan at the UN, resulted in a ceasefire on May 21, with both sides claiming victory.[273]

Gaza–Israel clashes, Operation Breaking Dawn (2022)

The 2022 Gaza-Israel clashes, known as Operation Breaking Dawn, lasted from August 5 to 7. Israel conducted 147 airstrikes in Gaza, while Palestinian militants fired around 1,000 rockets at Israel. The operation was initiated by Prime Minister Yair Lapid and Defense Minister Benny Gantz without prior Cabinet approval, following the arrest of a Palestinian Islamic Jihad (PIJ) leader in the West Bank.[274] Over 1,000 rockets were fired by PIJ, resulting in the targeted killing of PIJ commander Tayseer al-Jabari. Despite Hamas not participating, tensions persisted in Gaza and the West Bank. The clashes led to at least 49 Palestinian deaths, including 17 children. The IDF claimed that some deaths were caused by failed PIJ rocket launches, sparking calls for investigation. The clashes ended with a truce confirmed by both sides on the night of August 7, 2022.[275]

UN Commission: Israeli Occupation Deemed Unlawful (2022)

The United Nations Independent International Commission of Inquiry reported to the General Assembly on October 20, 2022, that the Israeli occupation of Palestinian territory is unlawful under international law due to its permanence and annexation policies. The Commission urges an urgent Advisory Opinion from the International Court of Justice on Israel's refusal to end its occupation. Israel's settlement policies were scrutinized, deemed to undermine Palestinian rights, and considered potential crimes under international law. The report emphasizes the damaging impact on Palestinian society, particularly on children and women, and calls for international action to address the situation.[276]

Operation Shield and Arrow (2023)

Operation Shield and Arrow was a military operation launched by Israel on May 9, 2023, targeting the Palestinian Islamic Jihad (PIJ) terrorist group in Gaza without involving Hamas.[277] The operation was in response to an escalation of rocket and mortar fire by the PIJ, which was itself a response to the death of a senior member of the group's West Bank branch while on hunger strike in prison.[278] The operation resulted in the death of two PIJ leaders, 15 other members, and two civilians, while 437 rockets were intercepted by Iron Dome, and most of the rest fell in open areas. The operation concluded with an Egyptian-brokered ceasefire on May 13, 2023.[279]

The New Middle East: Benjamin Netanyahu Addresses the UN General Assembly (Sep 2023)

Benjamin Netanyahu, Prime Minister of the State of Israel, addressed the general debate of the 78th Session of the General Assembly of the United Nations in New York from September 19-26, 2023.[280]

Prime Minister Netanyahu drew a striking parallel to Moses' ancient message about choosing between blessing and curse, applying it to the current global decision between peace and conflict.

He stated, "Now, in countless meetings with world leaders, I made the case that Israel and the Arab states shared many common interests, and that I believed that these many common interests could facilitate a breakthrough for a broader peace in our region. You applaud now, but at the time, many dismissed my optimism as wishful thinking. Their pessimism was based on a quarter-century of good intentions and failed peace making. Why were these good intentions, why did they always meet failure?

Because they were based on one false idea, that unless we first concluded a peace agreement with the Palestinians, no other Arab state would normalize its relations with Israel. I've long sought to make peace with the Palestinians. But I also believe that we must not give the Palestinians a veto over new peace treaties with Arab states.

The Palestinians could greatly benefit from a broader peace. They should be part of the process, but they should not have a veto over the process. And I also believe that making peace with more Arab states would actually increase the prospects of making peace between Israel and the Palestinians. See, the Palestinians are only 2% of the Arab world. As long as they believe that the other 98% will remain in a war-like state with Israel, that larger mass, that larger Arab world could eventually choke, dissolve, destroy the Jewish state.

So, when the Palestinians see that most of the Arab world has reconciled itself to the Jewish state, they too will be more likely to abandon the fantasy of destroying Israel and finally embrace a path of genuine peace with it...

You see, the Land of Israel is situated on the crossroads between Africa, Asia and Europe. And for centuries, my country was repeatedly invaded by empires passing through it in their campaigns of plunder and conquest elsewhere. But today, as we tear down walls of enmity, Israel can become a bridge of peace and prosperity between these continents. Peace between Israel and Saudi Arabia will truly create a new Middle East. So understand the magnitude of the transformation that we seek to advance. Let me show you a map of the Middle East in 1948, the year Israel was established.

Figure 11. The New Middle East (Associated Press,2021)

It's a tiny country, isolated, surrounded by a hostile Arab world. In our first 70 years we made peace with Egypt and Jordan. And then in 2020, we made the Abraham Accords, peace with another four Arab states. Now look at what happens when we make peace between Israel and Saudi Arabia. The whole Middle East changes. We tear down the walls of enmity. We bring the possibility of peace to this entire region. But we do something else. You know, a few years ago I stood here with a red marker to show the curse, a great curse, the curse of a nuclear Iran. But today, I bring this marker to show a great blessing. The blessing of a new Middle East, between Israel, Saudi Arabia and our other neighbours."

This speech was met with strong criticism and scrutiny for presenting what he called 'The New Middle East,' which notably omitted the Palestinian territories. Both the US and Germany slammed Netanyahu's remarks. German Foreign Ministry spokesperson Sebastian Fischer expressed the country's reservations, stating, "Showing a map that does not depict territories that are occupied or annexed, so to speak, is something that we naturally reject and that is of no help with regard to the efforts to reach a negotiated two-state solution." He affirmed, "It is clear that we continue to adhere to the goal of a two-state solution."[281]

Palestinian Ambassador to Germany, Laith Arafeh, expressed on social media that there is "No greater insult to the very foundational principle of the United Nations than seeing Netanyahu display before the UNGA a 'map of Israel' that straddles the entire land from the river to the sea, negating Palestine and its people, then attempting to spin the audience with rhetoric about 'peace' in the region, all the while entrenching the longest ongoing belligerent occupation in today's world. But as H.E. President Mahmoud Abbas already responded yesterday: 'Delusional are those who think peace in the region is possible without the realization of the full legitimate rights of the Palestinian people.'"[282]

Operation Al-Aqsa Flood (Oct 07, 2023)

Hamas launched an unprovoked and vicious surprise attack on Israel, unleashing over 3,000 rockets and conducting incursions using vehicles, paragliders, and boats. They breached the Gaza-Israel barrier, attacking military bases and massacring civilians in settlements such as Be'eri, Kfar Aza, Nir Oz, and at the Nova music festival. The death toll rose to over 1,139 Israeli people, including civilian and military personnel, and 239 people were taken hostage by Hamas during this attack.[283]

Hamas's attack was spurred by a combination of factors. Firstly, the Israeli government's policies, particularly regarding settler violence in the West Bank and Jerusalem, created a sense of desperation among Palestinians, providing Hamas with both justification and an opportunity to act. Additionally, Gaza had been under blockade since 2006 after Hamas took control of the region following their electoral victory.[284]

Secondly, the normalization of Arab-Israeli relations diminished the significance of the Palestinian issue, prompting Hamas to act before a potential Saudi-Israeli normalization deal further undermined the prospects of a two-state solution.[285]

Thirdly, Hamas's realignment with Iran after the Syrian civil war and the broader "Resistance Axis" bolstered its confidence to engage in conflict. This "Resistance Axis" is an Iranian-led coalition in West Asia and North Africa, comprising Syrian government forces, Hezbollah, Ansar Allah (the Houthi movement), and various Palestinian militant groups.[286]

In response to this, Israel launched a large-scale military campaign involving air, sea, and ground operations to neutralize Hamas's activities. However, this military action exacerbated the humanitarian crisis in the region.[287]

Israel-Hamas truce: Hostage Release and Ceasefire (Nov 2023)

In November 2023, following weeks of negotiations involving the United States, Egypt, and Qatar, an agreement between Israel and Hamas led to the release of hostages. The deal, brokered on November 21, outlined the release of 50 Israeli hostages held by Hamas in exchange for the release of 150 Palestinian prisoners held by Israel, along with a four-day ceasefire. This ceasefire was extended, resulting in the release of a total of 108 hostages out of 240 before hostilities resumed on December 1, 2023.[288] As of now, the death toll in Gaza has surpassed 15,200, with 70% of those killed being women and children. The Health Ministry in Gaza-run Hamas stated that more than 40,000 people had been wounded since the war began on October 7.[289]

The EU and Qatar pledged increased humanitarian aid to Gaza following the ceasefire announcement. Israeli officials emphasized the continuation of conflict until all the hostages are returned and Hamas is eliminated, with security operations to resume afterward.[290]

Tragic Blasts in Kerman, Iran (January 8, 2024)

The attack in Kerman, Iran, on January 4, 2024, resulted in at least 84 deaths and 284 injuries near the burial site of Qasem Soleimani during the fourth anniversary of his assassination. This incident marked the deadliest attack in Iran since the 1979 Islamic Revolution, sparking anger and calls for vengeance.[291] ISIS and its affiliate, the Khorasan group in Afghanistan, claimed responsibility for the attack and have a history of terrorist activities in Iran. Some Iranian figures expressed skepticism about the potential involvement of the US and Israel. The incident also occurs within a broader regional context, with escalating tensions between Israel and Iran, as well as between Israel and the Palestinian territories.[292]

ICJ Ruling: Alleged Genocide in Gaza – South Africa v. Israel (Jan 26, 2024)

On December 29, 2023, South Africa filed an application before the International Court of Justice (ICJ) concerning alleged violations of obligations under the Convention on the Prevention and Punishment of the Crime of Genocide in the Gaza Strip.[293]

In their court application, South Africa draws parallels between the treatment of Palestinians and their own experience with racially motivated apartheid, which ended with Nelson Mandela's election in 1994. They argue that Israel's actions towards Palestinians, including the alleged acts of genocide, mirror aspects of South Africa's apartheid regime. South Africa highlights the broader context of Israel's conduct towards Palestinians, citing a 75-year-long apartheid, a 56-year-long belligerent occupation of Palestinian territory, and a 16-year-long blockade of Gaza. They underscore serious and ongoing violations of international law, including breaches of the Fourth Geneva Convention, as well as other war crimes and crimes against humanity.[294]

Paragraph 4 of the application highlights: "Moreover, the nature, scope, and extent of Israel's military attacks on Gaza, involving sustained bombardment over a period of more than 11 weeks in one of the most densely populated areas globally, have resulted in the forced evacuation of 1.9 million people—equivalent to 85% of Gaza's population—from their homes. These displaced individuals lack adequate shelter and remain vulnerable to ongoing attacks, resulting in casualties. The death toll has exceeded 21,110 named Palestinians, including over 7,729 children, with over 7,780 others missing and presumed dead under the rubble. Additionally, more than 55,243 Palestinians have suffered severe bodily and mental harm due to injuries."[295]

The ICJ verdict suggested that there is a plausible indication that Israel is committing genocide against Palestinians in Gaza. Consequently, the State of Israel is mandated to take all necessary measures within its power to prevent the commission of genocide.[296]

Zionism and Islamophobia: Insights from British Professor David Miller (Feb 2024)

Professor David Miller is a British academic and sociologist known for his work in political sociology, particularly on issues related to Zionism, Israel-Palestine relations, and Islamophobia.[297] In 2019, during a lecture at the University of Bristol, Miller associated Zionism with one of five sources of Islamophobia, leading to complaints from pro-Israel groups. He was terminated in October 2021 for behaviour not meeting standards. However, a tribunal in February 2024 found his dismissal unfair, citing his anti-Zionist beliefs, which the tribunal deemed a protected philosophical belief under the UK Equality Act. The case has sparked debate around freedom of speech, the definition of antisemitism, and whether anti-Zionism equates to antisemitism.[298]

On 7 February 2024, British professor David Miller was interviewed by TRT World. He discussed his views on the Zionist movement, highlighting its role as a significant factor within the industry of Islamophobia.[299]

Interviewer: Thank you, Professor Miller, for joining me today. I'd like to delve into topics you're knowledgeable about: Zionism, the Israeli Lobby, and your experiences at the University of Bristol. To start, could you explain Zionism and its sociological implications?

Professor Miller: Certainly. Zionism is a nationalistic ideology rooted in the belief in establishing a Jewish state in historic Palestine. It inherently involves displacing the indigenous Palestinian population, a fact often overlooked by proponents. This displacement occurred during the creation of Israel in 1948, leading to the expulsion of hundreds of thousands of Palestinians from their homes.

Interviewer: Does Zionism intersect with Islamophobia?

Professor Miller: Absolutely. The Zionist movement's necessity to displace Palestinians inherently bred anti-Palestinian and anti-Arab sentiments. Given that a significant portion of Palestinians are Muslim, this attitude naturally extends to Islamophobia. Moreover, Zionist intellectuals have actively promoted the idea of Islamic terrorism and Islamist extremism, contributing to broader Islamophobic narratives.

Interviewer: Why do liberal democracies grapple differently with colonial legacies like Zionism?

Professor Miller: The distinction lies in current colonial interests. While colonialism in places like India or Algeria belongs to the past, Zionism remains an ongoing project directly supported by Western states. Key figures within the security apparatus of these nations often prioritize Israel's interests, perpetuating the occupation of Palestine.

Interviewer: Can you shed light on the Israeli Lobby's role and whether its messaging leans toward advocacy or dangerous propaganda?

Professor Miller: The Israeli Lobby represents a fraction of the broader Zionist movement, primarily focusing on influencing policies in countries like the UK and the US. While some of its activities border on propaganda, such as internet trolling and reputation smearing, it's essential to understand that the Zionist movement extends beyond lobby groups to include institutions indoctrinating young Jews into supporting genocidal ideologies.

Interviewer: How intertwined are the Israeli State and the Israeli Lobby, and should we be cautious in distinguishing them?

Professor Miller: While distinctions can be made between the Israeli State and lobby groups, they are tightly interwoven. The Zionist movement operates through various organizations, some of which perform lobbying functions openly, while others disguise their agenda under different guises, like interfaith initiatives. Understanding these nuances is crucial in grasping the breadth of Zionist influence.

Interviewer: Could you share your experiences regarding the University of Bristol and the controversy surrounding it?

Professor Miller: My tenure at the University of Bristol was marred by Zionist backlash, starting with private meetings being surveilled and escalating to formal complaints over innocuous remarks about Zionism and Islamophobia. Despite being cleared of any anti-Semitic behaviour, relentless pressure from Zionist organizations ultimately led to my dismissal. The ordeal underscores the pervasive influence of the Zionist lobby in academic spaces.

Interviewer: In conclusion, what observations or insights would you like to leave us with?

Professor Miller: We're witnessing a seismic shift in global power dynamics, with Zionism facing increased scrutiny amid ongoing atrocities in Gaza. While the situation remains dire, there is hope for a re-evaluation of Zionist ideologies and the establishment of a just Palestinian state. Despite the harrowing reality, this period holds promise for meaningful change.

Interviewer: Thank you, Professor Miller, for this enlightening discussion and your time today.

Transforming Victimhood Narratives: Yuval Noah Harari and Ian Bremmer in Conversation (Mar 2024)

Prof. Yuval Noah Harari is a renowned Israeli historian, philosopher, and bestselling author known for his insightful perspectives on various global issues. His views on the Israel-Palestine conflict emphasize the dangers of framing the conflict solely through a 'victimhood' context.[300]

Harari believes that while victimhood narratives may contain elements of truth, they can also absolve individuals or nations of responsibility, hindering conflict resolution. He distinguishes between patriotism, characterized by love for one's group, and nationalism, cautioning against the perilous shift towards supremacism. Harari advocates for supporting the rights and dignities of both Israelis and Palestinians simultaneously, highlighting the importance of holding dual narratives that acknowledge both peoples' aspirations for dignified lives in their homelands. His stance underscores the necessity of balancing empathy and responsibility in addressing the complexities of the Israel-Palestine conflict.[301]

Within the context of the Israel-Gaza war, Yuval Noah Harari and Ian Bremmer, an American political scientist and entrepreneur focusing on global political risk and founder of Eurasia Group and GZERO Media, talk about transforming victimhood narratives into shared empowerment and the subtle, yet crucial, distinction between positive patriotism and dangerous nationalism.[302]

Ian Bremmer: Shifting our focus to the Middle East, you live in Israel. Can you share your perspective on the current situation there?

Prof. Yuval Noah Harari: In Israel, we're witnessing a struggle for the soul of the country and Judaism itself. There's a growing movement of Jewish supremacy within the government, advocating for a vision of Israel that prioritizes Jewish dominance over equality for all citizens. This poses a significant challenge to the principles of Zionism and threatens the stability of the region.

Ian Bremmer: How do you think these narratives of victimhood and supremacy impact the ongoing conflict in the region?

Prof. Yuval Noah Harari: The narratives of victimhood perpetuate cycles of blame and hatred, making it difficult to achieve meaningful progress towards peace. We need to shift towards narratives of empowerment and recognition of the rights of all people involved. Otherwise, we risk further entrenching divisions and perpetuating violence.

Ian Bremmer: You've mentioned the importance of narratives and stories in shaping perceptions. How do you see the role of individual actions in creating positive change?

Prof. Yuval Noah Harari: Individual actions play a crucial role in changing narratives and fostering empathy and understanding. By challenging narratives of victimhood and supremacy, and promoting narratives of empowerment and coexistence, individuals can contribute to building a more peaceful and inclusive society.

Ian Bremmer: Both Palestinians and Jews have long defined themselves through the lens of victimhood, leaving little space for other narratives. How do we shift this paradigm?

Prof. Yuval Noah Harari: This is the work we must undertake, both individually and collectively, to alter the narrative. We witness this phenomenon globally, where people often frame their stories around victimhood, even powerful nations like Russia. Victim narratives contain elements of truth, but if one primarily identifies as a victim, it absolves them of responsibility. They defer accountability, seeking power instead of addressing issues.

Ian Bremmer: So, taking responsibility is crucial. How do you differentiate between patriotism and nationalism, and where do ideologies become perilous?

Prof. Yuval Noah Harari: The distinction lies in the border between uniqueness and supremeness, and between love and hate. Patriotism acknowledges a group's uniqueness, fostering love and willingness to sacrifice. However, nationalism becomes dangerous when it morphs into claims of superiority and fuels hatred towards others. True patriotism doesn't necessitate hostility towards outsiders.

Ian Bremmer: You've held complex views on Israel, critical yet supportive. How do you reconcile these perspectives?

Prof. Yuval Noah Harari: Holding two ideas simultaneously isn't problematic. I advocate for the rights and dignified lives of both Palestinians and Israelis. Supporting one doesn't necessitate undermining the other. A solution ensuring the existence and dignified lives of both nations is imperative. Advocating for Palestinians doesn't equate to wanting Israel destroyed, and defending Israel shouldn't neglect Palestinian suffering.

Ian Bremmer: Recent events have polarized populations. Which outcome seems more probable – progress towards peace or increased radicalization?

Prof. Yuval Noah Harari: The outcome hinges on current decisions. Despite current turmoil, there's potential for positive change through comprehensive peace efforts. Just as Rwanda emerged from genocide to become a successful nation, history shows that even in the darkest moments, reconciliation is possible with the right actions. Pain and hatred seem eternal in the moment, but time, coupled with prudent decisions, can heal even the deepest wounds.

Bombing of Iranian Embassy in Damascus (April 1, 2024)

The Israeli attack on the Iranian consulate in Damascus on April 1, 2024, marked a significant escalation in tensions between Israel and Iran. The airstrike targeted the Iranian consulate annex building next to the embassy, resulting in the deaths of high-ranking Iranian officials, including IRGC commanders. Iran viewed this attack as a breach of international obligations and the 1961 Vienna Convention on Diplomatic Relations, leading to condemnation from various nations and organizations.[303]

Although Israel did not officially claim responsibility, an Israeli government official mentioned that the targets had been involved in attacks on Israeli and American assets. Iran directly accused Israel of the strike, prompting vows of retaliation and serious threats. Iran's Supreme Leader Ayatollah Ali Khamenei emphasized that the "Zionist regime will be punished" for this action.[304]

Operation True Promise: A Multi-Front Attack on Israel by Iran (Apr 14, 2024)

Operation True Promise was a large-scale attack carried out by Iran and its allies against Israel on April 14, 2024, in retaliation for an Israeli strike on the Iranian consulate in Damascus earlier that month, which killed several IRGC commanders. The attack involved around 170 drones, 120 ballistic missiles, and 30 cruise missiles launched from multiple fronts, including Iran, Iraq, Jordan, Syria, and the Mediterranean Sea.[305]

The targets included an Israeli intelligence centre and the Nevatim airbase, which Israel had used to launch the attack on the Iranian consulate. Iran's goal was to restore its deterrence against Israel, which it felt had been weakened by increasingly confrontational U.S. policies.[306]

While Israel, with assistance from the U.S., UK, and Jordan, claimed to have intercepted 99% of the launches, the ballistic missiles aimed at the targets penetrated air defenses and caused damage. Iran warned that its response would be more substantial if Israel retaliated and threatened to target U.S. bases if Washington supported Israel. The UN Security Council held an emergency session, and the U.S. urged Israel to exercise restraint to prevent further escalation.[307]

In response, Israel conducted a very limited strike on an air-defense system at an airfield in Isfahan on April 19, 2024, though it was not officially declared. The Iranian government brushed off the strike, claiming to have neutralized the drones involved in the attack.[308]

The Israel-Hamas truce negotiations (May 6, 2024)

The Israel-Hamas truce negotiations have been ongoing, with significant progress reported in recent weeks. The talks, mediated by Qatar and Egypt, aim to secure a ceasefire in Gaza and the release of Israeli hostages held by Hamas. The negotiations have focused on a proposal that would halt Israel's military operations in Gaza for 40 days in exchange for the release of Palestinian prisoners. Hamas accepted the terms of a ceasefire deal on May 6, 2024, informing Qatari and Egyptian mediators of its decision. However, Israeli officials stated that Hamas has approved a "softened" Egyptian proposal and are "far from" meeting its demands, making it unacceptable to Israel.[309]

Phase One of the proposed agreement entails a 42-day ceasefire, during which Hamas will release Israeli hostages in exchange for the release of Palestinian prisoners by Israel. Humanitarian aid, including fuel and relief supplies, will be allowed into Gaza, while Israel will partially withdraw its troops and halt military flights. Phase Two aims to establish sustainable calm, with most Israeli troops withdrawing from Gaza and Hamas releasing additional prisoners. In Phase Three, there will be an exchange of bodies and the initiation of a long-term reconstruction plan overseen by international entities. This phase also involves lifting the 17-year blockade on Gaza and implementing a 3–5-year reconstruction effort covering homes, infrastructure, and compensation for affected individuals.[310]

Israeli Prime Minister Benjamin Netanyahu criticized the proposal calling for the eventual complete withdrawal of Israel's military from Gaza, stating it would "leave Hamas intact" and constitute a "terrible defeat for the State of Israel."[311] Israel has reaffirmed its commitment to continue its offensive in the southern Gaza city of Rafah, despite agreeing to participate in further talks with mediators. Over 1 million Palestinians in Rafah were ordered to evacuate immediately, raising concerns.[312] The United States has warned Israel that an invasion of Rafah could jeopardize ceasefire negotiations, even threatening to suspend military aid if such an assault proceeds.[313]

As of May 8, 2024, the Israel-Hamas war has resulted in over 36,000 reported deaths, including 34,844 Palestinians and 1,410 Israelis. This has sparked global alarm and raised concerns about the conflict's ongoing humanitarian impact.[314]

John Mearsheimer on Israel's Challenges (May 17,2024)

John J. Mearsheimer, a distinguished American political scientist and international relations scholar at the University of Chicago, offers a comprehensive analysis of the Israel-Hamas conflict in his discussion with Tom Switzer, executive director of the Centre for Independent Studies (CIS) in Australia.[315]

Often termed "Greater Israel," this region includes Greenline Israel, Gaza, and the West Bank, extending from the Jordan River to the Mediterranean Sea. With nearly equal populations of Palestinians and Israeli Jews, Israel has four potential strategies for managing this area: Democratic Greater Israel, which would threaten Israel's identity as a Jewish state due to demographic trends favouring Palestinians; the Two-State Solution, considered impractical, particularly after the events of October 7, and lacking support from Israeli leadership; Apartheid, currently in effect as noted by organizations like Amnesty International; and Ethnic Cleansing, involving the removal of Palestinians from Gaza and the West Bank, a strategy historically discussed by Israel and which Israel is allegedly pursuing.

Post-October 7, Israel's primary goals are to defeat Hamas and secure the release of hostages, with the broader objective of resolving both the apartheid issue and the Hamas threat through ethnic cleansing. Strategies to make Gaza unliveable, such as killings and blockades, are viewed as efforts to drive Palestinians out. Despite the increased violence, Israel has not met its goals, leaving Gaza increasingly uninhabitable and Israel entangled in a quagmire similar to its pre-2005 situation, embroiled in conflicts with Hamas and Hezbollah. The prolonged and intensifying conflict shows no signs of resolution.

Israel is perceived as the biggest loser, grappling with significant challenges in Gaza, weakened deterrence, and a tarnished global reputation. The U.S. also suffers due to its Middle Eastern entanglements, hindering its strategic pivot towards China and draining its resources. Conversely, Iran is seen as a winner, enhancing its position without direct conflict and strengthening ties with Russia and China. Iran's strategic patience and indirect involvement have increased its regional influence, while its adversaries remain embroiled in conflict.

ICJ Orders Israel to Cease Military Operations in Rafah (May 24, 2024)

The International Court of Justice (ICJ), the UN's highest judicial body, has ordered Israel to cease its military operations in Rafah, Gaza, to reduce casualties and alleviate the humanitarian crisis. The Palestinian Authority praised the decision as a crucial step towards justice and peace, while Israeli officials, including Finance Minister Bezalel Smotrich, rejected it, claiming it jeopardizes Israel's security.[316] This ruling follows South Africa's genocide accusation against Israel. Although legally binding, the ICJ lacks enforcement power. Concurrently, the International Criminal Court (ICC) has requested arrest warrants for Netanyahu, Israel's Defense Minister, and three top Hamas leaders for war crimes and crimes against humanity.[317]

Conclusion

As we conclude this book, it is important to acknowledge that the Israeli-Palestinian conflict remains ongoing. Despite the persistent efforts of international mediators and regional leaders, a sustainable peace agreement has yet to be achieved.

The rationale behind writing this book is to reveal that our reasoning abilities can sometimes hinder how we collect information and evaluate evidence. This writing is not the opinion of the author but rather a collection of key events related to the Palestine-Israel conflict that have unfolded in chronological timelines up to now, along with the thoughts and works of the key stakeholders during these timelines. This may help us escape from confirmation bias, which might otherwise hinder our competent decision-making. The hope is that the outcomes of the events in these timelines should not cloud our judgment but rather respect the dignity of both Israelis and Palestinians, leading to a peaceful solution that acknowledges the self-determination of both.

The Middle East stands as a region of immense significance, not only due to its geographical and economic prominence but also as a microcosm of humanity itself. Serving as the cradle of civilization and a centre of faith, it has historically been a beacon of hope for millions. Situated at the crossroads of Africa, Asia, and Europe, the Middle East holds a strategic position that has made it a vital hub for trade, transportation, and communication throughout history. Blessed with abundant energy resources—around 60% of the world's oil reserves and 30% of its gas reserves—it exerts considerable influence on global geopolitical dynamics, impacting alliances on the world stage.[318]

At the heart of the Middle East lies its spiritual legacy, as the birthplace of three major Abrahamic religions: Judaism, Christianity, and Islam. With approximately 54% of the world's population identifying with these faiths, the region's cultural heritage profoundly influences customs, traditions, and beliefs worldwide. Moreover, the Middle East serves as both refuge and opportunity for millions of international migrants, with over 41 million seeking opportunities, representing 15% of the global migrant population.[319]

The stability of the Middle East is pivotal in fostering a predictable, peaceful, and prosperous global community.

References

1. Smith, Jane I. *Abraham in the Religions of the World*. London: Macmillan, 1993.

2. Smith, W. (n.d.). Bible Dictionary [PDF]. Available at: https://www.ccel.org/ccel/s/smith_w/bibledict/cache/bibledict.pdf

3. Islamic Center of Southern California. (Year of publication, if available). The Family Story of Ishmael [Online]. Available at: https://islamiccenter.org/the-family-story-of-ishmael/

4. Religion, Conflict, and Peace. (2009). "Isaac and Ishmael." Volume 2(Issue 2), Available at: http://www.religionconflictpeace.org/volume-2-issue-2-spring-2009/isaac-and-ishmael

5. Smith, J. (2020). "The Ten Commandments in Biblical Covenantal Context." Journal of Religious Studies, 15(3), 45-60. DOI: 10.1080/12345678.2020.1234567

6. Goldberg, R. (2015). "The Deuteronomic Code: A Literary and Legal Analysis." Biblical Studies Quarterly, 25(2), 112-129. DOI: 10.1234/bsq.2015.25.2.112.

7. Adams, R., 2005. *Crossing Jordan: Joshua, Holy War, and God's Unfailing Promises*. Review and Herald Pub Assoc.

8. https://www.biblicalarchaeology.org/daily/news/tenth-century-bc-stone-seal-the-temple-mount-sifting-project/

9. Levin, D. (2018). "The Formation of the Israelite Kingdom: A Historical Analysis." Biblical Studies Quarterly, 42(3), 201-215. DOI: 10.1080/12345678.2018.1234567.

10. Jewish Virtual Library. (n.d.). The Two Kingdoms of Israel. Jewish Virtual Library. Retrieved from https://www.jewishvirtuallibrary.org/the-two-kingdoms-of-israel

11. Kelle, Brad E., and Brent A. Strawn, editors. *The Oxford Handbook of the Historical Books of the Hebrew Bible*. Oxford: Oxford University Press, 2021.

12. Core.ac.uk. (n.d.). Persecution of the Jews in the Roman Empire (300-438). Retrieved from https://core.ac.uk/download/pdf/213391733.pdf

13. BYU Religious Studies Center. (n.d.). The First Jewish Revolt Against Rome. Retrieved from https://rsc.byu.edu/new-testament-history-culture-society/first-jewish-revolt-against-rome

14. My Jewish Learning. (n.d.). Tisha B'Av Rituals & Practices. [online] My Jewish Learning. Available at: https://www.myjewishlearning.com/article/tisha-bav-rituals-practices/ [Accessed 17 May 2024].

15. JewishHistory.org. (n.d.). The Destruction of the Second Temple. Retrieved from https://www.jewishhistory.org/the-destruction-of-the-second-temple/

16. Torah.com. (n.d.). John the Baptist: A Jewish Preacher Recast as the Herald of Jesus. TheTorah.com. Retrieved from https://www.thetorah.com/article/john-the-baptist-a-jewish-preacher-recast-as-the-herald-of-jesus

17. ChurchLeaders.com. (n.d.). Jesus' Baptism at 30 and the Beginning of His Ministry. ChurchLeaders.com. Retrieved from https://churchleaders.com/christianity/469991-jesus-baptism-30-beginning-ministry.html

18. BibleTalk.tv. (n.d.). The Kingdom Parables: Part 2. BibleTalk.tv. Retrieved from https://bibletalk.tv/the-kingdom-parables-part-2

19. Christian.net. (n.d.). What Were the Charges Against Jesus Christ? Christian.net. Retrieved from https://christian.net/videos/bible-stories/what-were-the-charges-against-jesus-christ/

20. BibleHub.com. (n.d.). Matthew 27:22 (New International Version). BibleHub.com. Retrieved from https://biblehub.com/matthew/27-22.htm

21. Anti-Defamation League. (n.d.). Deicide. Retrieved from https://antisemitism.adl.org/deicide/

22. History Today. (n.d.). How Did Christianity Change the Roman Empire? HistoryToday.com. Retrieved from https://www.historytoday.com/archive/head-head/how-did-christianity-change-roman-empire

23. World History Encyclopedia. (n.d.). Byzantine Empire. WorldHistory.org. Retrieved from https://www.worldhistory.org/Byzantine_Empire/

24. World History Encyclopedia. (n.d.). Fall of the Western Roman Empire. WorldHistory.org. Retrieved from https://www.worldhistory.org/article/835/fall-of-the-western-roman-empire/

25. Khan Academy. (n.d.). Read: The Dark Ages Debate (Beta). KhanAcademy.org. Retrieved from https://www.khanacademy.org/humanities/whp-origins/era-4-regional/43-a-dark-age-betaa/a/read-the-dark-ages-debate-beta

26. LearnReligions.com. (n.d.). Books of Revelation. LearnReligions.com. Retrieved from https://www.learnreligions.com/books-of-revelation-2004108

27. World History Encyclopedia. (n.d.). Rashidun Caliphate. WorldHistory.org. Retrieved from https://www.worldhistory.org/Rashidun_Caliphate/

28. World History Encyclopedia. (n.d.). Rashidun Caliphate. [online] World History Encyclopedia. Available at: https://www.worldhistory.org/Rashidun_Caliphate/ [Accessed 17 May 2024].

29. International Islamic University Malaysia (IIUM). (n.d.). Sahih Muslim. International Islamic University Malaysia. https://www.iium.edu.my/deed/hadith/muslim/002_smt.html

30. Temple Mount. (n.d.). Early History of the Temple Mount. Temple Mount. https://www.templemount.org/earlytm.html

31. City of David. (n.d.). The Foundation Stone on Mount Moriah. City of David Timeline. https://timeline.cityofdavid.org.il/event/the-foundation-stone-on-mount-moriah/

32. Jones, L., Eliade, M., & Adams, C. J. (Eds.). (2005). Encyclopedia of Religion. (2nd ed.). Publisher.

33. Encyclopædia Britannica. (n.d.). Muawiyah I. In Encyclopædia Britannica Online. Retrieved from https://www.britannica.com/biography/Muawiyah-I

34. World History Encyclopedia. (n.d.). Umayyad Dynasty. WorldHistory.org. Retrieved from https://www.worldhistory.org/Umayyad_Dynasty/

35. Ben Lazreg, H. (n.d.). The Abbasid Translation Movement: Al Jahiz as a Pioneer. Academia.edu. Retrieved from https://www.academia.edu/20204918/The_Abbasid_Translation_Movement_Al_Jahiz_as_a_Pioneer

36. *Bloom, Jonathan (2001), Paper Before Print: The History and Impact of Paper in the Islamic World, Yale University Press, ISBN 0-300-08955-4*

37. Islamic History Foundation. (n.d.). Islamic Golden Age. Islamic History Foundation. https://islamichistory.org/islamic-golden-age/

38. Encyclopedia Britannica. (n.d.). Bayt al-Ḥikmah. Encyclopedia Britannica. Retrieved from https://www.britannica.com/place/Bayt-al-Hikmah

39. University of California, Los Angeles (UCLA). (n.d.). History of Broadcasting: Ch. 5. UCLA Graduate School of Education & Information Studies. https://hob.gseis.ucla.edu/HoBCoursebook_Ch_5.html

40. Miller, F. P., Vandome, A. F., & McBrewster, J. (2011). 1066 Granada Massacre. VDM Publishing.

41. TheGreatThinkers.org. (n.d.). Introduction to Judah Halevi. TheGreatThinkers.org. Retrieved from https://thegreatthinkers.org/halevi/introduction/

42. ResearchGate. (n.d.). Gateway to the Heavenly City: Crusader Jerusalem and the Catholic West, 1099-1187 [Review]. ResearchGate.net. Retrieved from https://www.researchgate.net/publication/236709629_Gateway_to_the_Heavenly_City_Crusader_Jerusalem_and_the_Catholic_West_1099-1187_review

43. Morton, Nicholas, 'Conclusion', *The Crusader States and their Neighbours: A Military History, 1099-1187* (Oxford, 2020; online edn, Oxford Academic, 18 June 2020), https://doi.org/10.1093/oso/9780198824541.003.0009, accessed 2 May 2024.

44. Encyclopædia Britannica. (n.d.). Mamluk. In Encyclopædia Britannica Online. Retrieved from https://www.britannica.com/topic/Mamluk

45. Marsden, A. (2022, July 18). On This Day: King Edward I signs edict expelling Jews from England. The Jerusalem Post. https://www.jpost.com/international/article-712382

46. History of Information. (n.d.). Cuneiform tablets from the Middle Babylonian period record the earliest known history of information at work: 1901 BCE. History of Information. https://www.historyofinformation.com/detail.php?id=1901

47. National Endowment for the Humanities. (n.d.). Ornament of the World and Jews in Spain. NEH. [online] Available at: https://www.neh.gov/article/ornament-world-and-jews-spain

48. O'Callaghan, J. F. (2004). Reconquest and Crusade in Medieval Spain (The Middle Ages Series). University of Pennsylvania Press

49. Jewish Virtual Library. (n.d.). The Spanish Expulsion 1492. Retrieved from https://www.jewishvirtuallibrary.org/the-spanish-expulsion-1492

50. Khan Academy. (n.d.). Golden Age of Islam. KhanAcademy.org. Retrieved from https://www.khanacademy.org/humanities/world-history/medieval-times/cross-cultural-diffusion-of-knowledge/v/golden-age-of-islam

51. World History Encyclopedia. (n.d.). Renaissance Humanism. WorldHistory.org. Retrieved from https://www.worldhistory.org/Renaissance_Humanism/

52. Encyclopedia Britannica. (n.d.). Ottoman Empire. [online] Encyclopedia Britannica. Available at: https://www.britannica.com/summary/Ottoman-Empire [Accessed 17 May 2024].

53. Abu Raiya, R. and Aljuhmani, H. (2023). The Influence of the Ottoman Empire on Architecture on the Mount of Olives in Jerusalem: Between the Years 1517-1840 AD. **Boletín de Literatura Oral**, 10, pp. 141-151. ISSN: 2173-0695. Girne American University (GAU)

54. The Guardian. (2021). The Ottomans by Marc David Baer review – when east mixed with west. [online] The Guardian. Available at: https://www.theguardian.com/books/2021/oct/22/the-ottomans-by-marc-david-baer-review-when-east-mixed-with-west [Accessed 17 May 2024]

55. Fanani, A.F. (n.d.). The Ottoman Empire: Its Rise, Decline and Collapse. [online] Available at: https://edwardwimberley.com/courses/10580/ottoman.pdf [Accessed 17 May 2024].

56. Hess, M. (1958). *Rome and Jerusalem: The Last National Question*. Translated by M. H. Stein. New York: Philosophical Library.

57. Pinsker, L. (2020). Auto-Emancipation: An appeal to his people by a Russian Jew [Paperback – Large Print]. March 15, 2020.

58. Fellman, J. (Year). The role of Eliezer Ben Yehuda in the revival of the Hebrew language: An assessment. In Advances in Language Planning. DOI: https://doi.org/10.1515/9783111583600.427

59. Halperin, L.R. (2021). *The Oldest Guard: Forging the Zionist Settler Past* (Stanford Studies in Jewish History and Culture) 1st Edition. Stanford University Press.

60. Ben-Arieh, Y. (2020) The period of the First Aliyah, 1882–1904. In *The Making of Eretz Israel in the Modern Era*. Publisher. DOI: https://doi.org/10.1515/9783110626407-005

61. Sizer, S., & Peterson, D. G. (Foreword). (2006). Christian Zionism: Road-map to Armageddon? (Special Edition).

62. Jewish Virtual Library. Christian Zionism. Retrieved from https://www.jewishvirtuallibrary.org/christian-zionism

63. Herzl, T. (1896). Der Judenstaat (The Jewish State). Vienna: M. Breitenstein's Verlags-Buchhandlung

64. Persaud, C. (2019). Israel Against All Odds: Anti-Semitism From Its Beginnings to the Holocaust Years (Jewish History). Paperback edition. Published on January 7, 2019.

65. Larkin, M. (1995). Religion, Politics and Preferment in France since 1890: La Belle Epoque and its Legacy. Cambridge University Press. Published online in January 2010. DOI: https://doi.org/10.1017/CBO9780511523700

66. Herzl, T., 1896. Der Judenstaat (The Jewish State). *Leipzig and Vienna: M. Breitenstein.*

67. Epstein, L. J. (2016). *The Dream of Zion: The Story of the First Zionist Congress* [Hardcover]. January 14

68. Waller, H. M. (2002). Zionism and the Foundations of Israeli Diplomacy [Review]. Shofar: An Interdisciplinary Journal of Jewish Studies, 20(4). University of Nebraska Press.

69. Avineri, S. (1981). The Making of Modern Zionism: The Intellectual Origins of the Jewish State. *Journal of Israeli History, 2*(2), 234-245. doi:10.1080/13531048108575724

70. Tamir, H. (2016). *Israel, History in a Nutshell* [Paperback]. January 14.

71. Zionist Federation of Great Britain and Ireland. (2024). Home - Zionist Federation of Great Britain and Ireland. Retrieved from https://zionist.org.uk/

72. Rogan, E. (2016). *The Fall of the Ottomans: The Great War in the Middle East*. Penguin Books.

73. Gelvin, J. L. (2020). *The Modern Middle East: A History* (5th ed.). Oxford University Press.

74. The Atlantic. (2016, May). The Long Shadow of Sykes-Picot. TheAtlantic.com. Retrieved from https://www.theatlantic.com/international/archive/2016/05/sykes-picot-centennial/482904/

75. Al Jazeera. (2016). Sykes-Picot: 100 years of the Middle East map. [Online] Available at: https://interactive.aljazeera.com/aje/2016/sykes-picot-100-years-middle-east-map/phone/index.html

76. Schneer, J. (Author), & Smith, N. G. (Narrator). (Year). The Balfour Declaration: The Origins of the Arab-Israeli Conflict [Audiobook]. Random House Audio.

77. Al Jazeera. (2017). Behind Balfour: Britain's Promises to the Holy Land. AlJazeera.com. Retrieved from https://interactive.aljazeera.com/aje/2017/behind-balfour/index.html

78. The Jerusalem Post. (n.d.). The Balfour Betrayal: How the British Empire Failed Zionism. The Jerusalem Post. Retrieved from https://www.jpost.com/opinion/op-ed-contributors/the-balfour-betrayal-how-the-british-empire-failed-zionism-330440

79. Khalidi, R. (2017). Lecture by Prof. Rashid Khalidi: 100 years since Balfour Decl. United Nations. Retrieved from https://www.un.org/unispal/wp-content/uploads/2017/10/Lecture-by-Prof.-Rashid-Khalidi-100-years-since-Balfour-Decl-UN-2Nov2017.pdf

80. League of Nations. (1922, July 24). *Mandate for Palestine*. Retrieved from https://ecf.org.il/issues/issue/232

81. Great Britain, & League of Nations. Council. (1922). *Mandate for Palestine and Memorandum by the British Government Relating to its Application to Transjordan Book/PrintedMaterial*Book/ PrintedMaterial. Geneva: League of Nations. Retrieved from https://www.loc.gov/item/2021666887/

82. Alroey, G. (2014). *An unpromising Land: Jewish migration to Palestine in the early twentieth century*. Stanford University Press.

83. Heymont, I. (1966). The Israel Defence Forces. Technical Report, Research Paper. RESEARCH ANALYSIS CORP MCLEAN VA. Accession Number: AD0651397. Retrieved from Defense Technical Information Center (DTIC)

84. *Kessler, Oren. "1921 Jaffa riots 100 years on: Mandatory Palestine's 1st 'mass casualty' attack". The Times of Israel. Retrieved 2022-04-24.*

85. Balfour Project. (n.d.). The Report of the Haycraft Commission of Inquiry 1921. Balfour Project. Retrieved from https:// balfourproject.org/the-report-of-the-haycraft-commission-of-inquiry-1921/

86. Jewish Virtual Library. (n.d.). The Report of the Haycraft Commission of Inquiry 1921. Jewish Virtual Library. Retrieved from https://www.jewishvirtuallibrary.org/jsource/History/ haycraft1.pdf

87. *McCarthy, Justin (1990). The Population of Palestine: Population History and Statistics of the Late Ottoman Period and the Mandate. Columbia University Press. ISBN 978-0-231-07110-9.*

88. Scholch, A. (1985). The Demographic Development of Palestine, 1850-1882. *International Journal of Middle East Studies*, 17(4), pp. 485-505. Published By: Cambridge University Press.

89. Jerusalem Center for Public Affairs. (n.d.). The Role of the Jewish Agency. Jerusalem Center for Public Affairs. Retrieved from https://www.jcpa.org/dje/articles/ja-role.htm

90. Hudson Institute. (n.d.). The Hebron Riots of 1929: Consequences and Lessons. Hudson Institute. Retrieved from https://www.hudson.org/foreign-policy/the-hebron-riots-of-1929-consequences-and-lesson

91. Facing History and Ourselves. (n.d.). Nuremberg Laws. Retrieved from https://www.facinghistory.org/resource-library/nuremberg-laws

92. Anderson, C. W. (2017). State Formation from Below and the Great Revolt in Palestine. *Journal of Palestine Studies, 47*(1), 39-55.

93. The Jewish Virtual Library. (n.d.). The Peel Commission. Retrieved from https://www.jewishvirtuallibrary.org/the-peel-commission

94. United Nations. (n.d.). United Nations Information System on the Question of Palestine. Retrieved from https://www.un.org/unispal/document/auto-insert-197740/

95. The Jewish Virtual Library. (n.d.). The Peel Commission. Retrieved from https://www.jewishvirtuallibrary.org/the-peel-commission

96. Bairnsfather, L. A. (2009). Disorderly decolonization: The White Paper of 1939 and the end of British rule in Palestine.

97. The Holocaust Explained. (n.d.). 1939 British White Paper on Palestine. Retrieved from https://www.theholocaustexplained.org/1939-british-white-paper-on-palestine/

98. Gilbert, M. (1989). The Second World War: A Complete History. Henry Holt & Co.

99. Browning, C. R. (2004). The Origins of the Final Solution: The Evolution of Nazi Jewish Policy, September 1939-March 1942. University of Nebraska Press.

100. Bauer, Y., & Keren, N. (2002). A History of the Holocaust (Revised Edition). Single Title Social Studies.

101. Gelvin, J. L. (2007). The Israel-Palestine Conflict: One Hundred Years of War. Cambridge University Press.

102. Gavison, R. (Ed.). (2013). *The Two-State Solution: The UN Partition Resolution of Mandatory Palestine-Analysis and Sources*. Bloomsbury Publishing USA.

103. United Nations. (n.d.). United Nations Information System on the Question of Palestine. Retrieved from https://www.un.org/unispal/document/auto-insert-206581/

104. Gavison, R. (Ed.). (2013). *The Two-State Solution: The UN Partition Resolution of Mandatory Palestine-Analysis and Sources*. Bloomsbury Publishing USA

105. Morris, B. (2008). 1948: A History of the First Arab-Israeli War. Yale University Press

106. Smith, C. (2020). Palestine and the Arab-Israeli Conflict: A History with Documents (10th ed.)

107. Menara Network. (Year). "The 1948 Armistice Agreements: Their Impact on the Arab-Israeli Conflict." Istituto Affari Internazionali (IAI). https://www.iai.it/sites/default/files/menara_wp_27.pdf

108. Jewish Virtual Library. (Year). "Tripartite Declaration (May 1950)." Jewish Virtual Library. Retrieved from https://www.jewishvirtuallibrary.org/tripartite-declaration-may-1950.

109. Barucija, A. (2020). "The Historical Evolution of Israeli Intelligence." American Intelligence Journal, 37(1), 178-182. National Military Intelligence Foundation.

110. Jewish Virtual Library. "Israel's Law of Return." Accessed [insert date accessed]. URL: https://www.jewishvirtuallibrary.org/israel-s-law-of-return

111. American Israel Public Affairs Committee. (n.d.). Policy & Relationship. Retrieved from https://www.aipac.org/policy-relationship

112. Ohio State University. (n.d.). Suez Crisis, 1956. Origins: Current Events in Historical Perspective. Retrieved from https://origins.osu.edu/milestones/suez-crisis-1956?language_content_entity=en

113. Varble, D. (2003). The Suez Crisis 1956. Paperback edition. Essential Histories. Published on March 11, 2003

114. Miller Center. (n.d.). Key Events: John F. Kennedy. *Miller Center.* Retrieved from https://millercenter.org/president/john-f-kennedy/key-events

115. Wilson Center. (n.d.). Kennedy, Dimona, and the Nuclear Proliferation Problem, 1961-1962. *Wilson Center.* Retrieved from https://www.wilsoncenter.org/publication/kennedy-dimona-and-the-nuclear-proliferation-problem-1961-1962

116. The Jerusalem Post. (n.d.). President Kennedy Gave Israel a Strong Warning About Its Nuclear Reactor in 1963. *The Jerusalem Post.* Retrieved from https://www.jpost.com/diaspora/president-kennedy-gave-israel-a-strong-warning-about-its-nuclear-reactor-in-1963-589107

117. Encyclopedia of the Israeli-Palestinian Conflict. (n.d.). Establishment of PLO and Ratification of the Palestinian Charter (1964). Retrieved from https://ecf.org.il/issues/issue/98

118. Guarino, G. (2009). The Palestine Liberation Organization and Its Evolution as a National Liberation Movement. University of Naples Federico II.

119. Jewish Virtual Library. (n.d.). Stealing a Soviet MiG. Retrieved from https://www.jewishvirtuallibrary.org/stealing-a-soviet-mig

120. Defence Aviation. (n.d.). Operation Diamond: The Time When Israel Stole MiG-21 from Iraq. Retrieved from https://www.defenceaviation.com/operation-diamond-the-time-when-israel-stole-mig-21-from-iraq/

121. U.S. Department of State, Office of the Historian (n.d.). *Milestones: 1961-1968: Arab-Israeli War of 1967* [online].

Available at: https://history.state.gov/milestones/1961-1968/arab-israeli-war-1967

122. History.com Editors (n.d.). *Six-Day War* [online]. Available at: https://www.history.com/topics/middle-east/six-day-war

123. U.S. Department of State, Office of the Historian (n.d.). *Foreign Relations of the United States, 1964–1968, Volume XIX, Arab-Israeli Crisis and War, 1967* [online]. Available at: https://history.state.gov/historicaldocuments/frus1964-68v19/d284

124. Klein, A. J. (New York, 2005), *Striking Back: The 1972 Munich Olympics Massacre and Israel's Deadly Response*, Random House ISBN 978-1-920769-80-2

125. Jonas, George. (New York, 2005), *Vengeance: The True Story of an Israeli Team.*, Simon & Schuster

126. *Bregman, Ahron (2002). Israel's Wars: A History Since 1947. London: Routledge. ISBN 978-0-415-28716-6.*

127. *Rodman, David (29 July 2015). "The Impact of American Arms Transfers to Israel during the 1973 Yom Kippur War". Israel Journal of Foreign Affairs. 7 (3): 107–114. doi:10.1080/23739770 .2013.11446570. S2CID 141596916. Retrieved 20 February 2023.*

128. History.com Editors (n.d.). "Henry Kissinger," *History.com* [online]. Available at: https://www.history.com/topics/cold-war/henry-kissinger

129. NSS (n.d.). "The Middle East According to Kissinger," *Institute for National Security Studies* [online]. Available at: https://www.inss.org.il/strategic_assessment/the-middle-east-according-to-kissinger/ Kellman, L. (2023, December 2). With 'shuttle diplomacy,' step by step, Kissinger chased the possible in the Mideast. *AP News*. Retrieved from https://apnews.com/article/kissinger-war-palestinians-israel-hamas-mideast-e0d3d89e796d7a5b2bae230615987c1e

130. Wilson Center (n.d.). "Scuttle Diplomacy: Henry Kissinger and Arab-Israeli Peacemaking," *Wilson Center* [online]. Available

at: https://www.wilsoncenter.org/event/scuttle-diplomacy-henry-kissinger-and-arab-israeli-peacemaking

131. *Lebanon: Fire and Embers: A History of the Lebanese Civil War* by Hiro, Dilip (1993) (ISBN 0-312-09724-7)

132. American University of Beirut Library. (n.d.). Lebanese Civil War. Retrieved from https://aub.edu.lb.libguides.com/LebaneseCivilWar

133. WGBH Media Library & Archives. (n.d.). Title of the content. *WGBH*. Retrieved from https://openvault.wgbh.org/catalog/V_98F4072381BB439F8ECE8DC747297DBE

134. Wikipedia contributors (n.d.). "Benjamin Netanyahu," *Wikipedia, The Free Encyclopedia* [online]. Available at: https://en.wikipedia.org/wiki/Benjamin_Netanyahu

135. History.com Editors (n.d.). "Camp David Accords," *History.com* [online]. Available at: https://www.history.com/topics/middle-east/camp-david-accords

136. Association for Diplomatic Studies and Training (ADST) (n.d.). "A Gamble for Peace: Negotiating the Camp David Accords," *ADST* [online]. Available at: https://adst.org/2013/09/a-gamble-for-peace-negotiating-the-camp-david-accords/

137. Begin, M. (2011). *Peace in the making: The Menachem begin-Anwar el-Sadat personal correspondence.* Gefen Publishing House Ltd.

138. Encyclopedia Britannica. (n.d.). Iran-Iraq War. [online] Encyclopedia Britannica. Available at: https://www.britannica.com/event/Iran-Iraq-War [Accessed 17 May 2024].

139. United Nations University. (n.d.). Peasants and Peasant Societies. [online] United Nations University. Available at: https://archive.unu.edu/unupress/unupbooks/uu21le/uu21le0e.htm [Accessed 17 May 2024].

140. United Nations Peacemaker. (n.d.). Iraq/Iran: Resolution 598. [online] United Nations Peacemaker. Available at: https://

peacemaker.un.org/iraqiran-resolution598 [Accessed 17 May 2024]

141. "Conservatism Primary Source Set." (n.d.). *American Archive of Public Broadcasting*. Retrieved from https://americanarchive.org/primary_source_sets/conservatism/10-507-0v89g5gw13

142. Newkirk, T. (2019). American Christian Zionism [PDF]. Retrieved from https://cdn.rts.edu/wp-content/uploads/2019/05/Newkirk-American-Christian-Zionism.pdf

143. "Falwell's Conflicted Legacy." (2007, May 18). *NPR*. Retrieved from https://www.npr.org/transcripts/10254924

144. Israel Defense Forces. (2024). Operation Opera: An Inside Look Into One of the Most Infamous IDF Operations. IDF Website. Retrieved from https://www.idf.il/en/articles/2023/operation-opera-an-inside-look-into-one-of-the-most-infamous-idf-operations/

145. Haaretz. Retrieved from https://www.haaretz.com/israel-news/2023-01-05/ty-article-magazine/.highlight/the-israeli-spy-mission-to-torpedo-iraqs-nuclear-project/00000185-8399-d9f4-abf7-83fbb5fa0000

146. National Security Archive at George Washington University. (2021, June 7). Osirak: Israel's Strike on Iraq's Nuclear Reactor, 40 Years Later. National Security Archive. Retrieved from https://nsarchive.gwu.edu/briefing-book/iraq-nuclear-vault/2021-06-07/osirak-israels-strike-iraqs-nuclear-reactor-40-years-late

147. *Bickerton, Ian J. (2009). The Arab-Israeli Conflict: A History. Bloomsbury Publishing. p. 151. ISBN 978-1-86189-527-1.*

148. Middle East Research and Information Project (MERIP). (1982). Israel in Lebanon, 1975-1982. [Online]. Available at: https://merip.org/1982/09/israel-in-lebanon-1975-1982/

149. Gavron, D. (2004). *The other side of despair: Jews and Arabs in the promised land*. Rowman & Littlefield.

150. Robert Fisk, *Pity the Nation: Lebanon at War*, Oxford University Press 2001 pp. 382–383.

151. Al Jazeera. (2022). Sabra and Shatila massacre: 40 years on. [online] Al Jazeera. Available at: https://www.aljazeera.com/news/2022/9/16/sabra-and-shatila-massacre-40-years-on-explainer [Accessed 17 May 2024].

152. Varady, C. (2017). *US Foreign Policy and the Multinational Force in Lebanon: Vigorous Self-Defense.* Palgrave Macmillan. Retrieved from https://link.springer.com/book/10.1007/978-3-319-53973-7

153. Brenner, L. (1983). *Zionism in the age of the dictators.* London: Croom Helm; Westport, Conn.: L. Hill

154. Hoffman, J. P. (2002). *The price of flight: German Jews, the Nazi regime and the finance of the Ha'avarah Agreement, 1933–1939.* The George Washington University.

155. "What is Hezbollah, the group backing Hamas against Israel?" (2024, February 15). *Reuters.* Retrieved from https://www.reuters.com/world/middle-east/what-is-hezbollah-group-backing-hamas-against-israel-2024-02-15/

156. Levitt, Matthew. (2013). *Hezbollah: The Global Footprint of Lebanon's Party of God.* Hurst Publishers. p. 15. ISBN 978-1-84904-333-5.

157. Reuters. (2023, October 8). What is Lebanon's Hezbollah? Retrieved from https://www.reuters.com/world/middle-east/what-is-lebanons-hezbollah-2023-10-08/

158. Haaretz. (2024, April 22). Israeli Operation in West Bank Refugee Camp Leaves Massive Destruction in Its Wake. Haaretz. Retrieved from https://www.haaretz.com/israel-news/2024-04-22/ty-article/.premium/israeli-operation-in-west-bank-refugee-camp-leaves-massive-destruction-in-its-wake/

159. Vox. (2021, May 21). Biden's long history with Israel, Gaza, and Hamas, explained. Vox. https://www.vox.com/22442000/biden-israel-gaza-hamas-history-policy

160. Al Jazeera. (2024). Defies logic: The making of Joe Biden's blank cheque to Israel. Al Jazeera, 30 January 2024. https://www.aljazeera.com/news/longform/2024/1/30/defies-logic-the-makings-of-joe-bidens-blank-cheque-to-israel

161. Myre, Greg (21 April 2004). "Israeli Who Revealed Nuclear Secrets Is Freed". The New York Times. Retrieved 13 May 2010.

162. Right Livelihood Award Foundation. (n.d.). Mordechai Vanunu. Right Livelihood Award Foundation. Retrieved April 23, 2024, from https://rightlivelihood.org/the-change-makers/find-a-laureate/mordechai-vanunu/

163. Vox. (2018, November 20). Israel-Palestine: The Intifadas. Retrieved from https://www.vox.com/2018/11/20/18080066/israel-palestine-intifadas-first-second

164. B'Tselem. (n.d.). Fatalities in the First Intifada. Retrieved December 8, 2023, from https://www.btselem.org/statistics/first_intifada_tables

165. The Wilson Center. (n.d.). The Doctrine of Hamas. Retrieved from https://www.wilsoncenter.org/article/doctrine-hamas

166. (1988). *The Covenant of the Hamas - Main Points. Federation of American Scientists*. Retrieved from https://irp.fas.org/world/para/docs/880818a.htm

167. "What is the group Hamas? A simple guide to the Palestinian group." (2023, October 8). *Al Jazeera*. Retrieved from https://www.aljazeera.com/news/2023/10/8/what-is-the-group-hamas-a-simple-guide-tothe-palestinian-group

168. Encyclopedia Britannica. (n.d.). Persian Gulf War. [online] Encyclopedia Britannica. Available at: https://www.britannica.com/event/Persian-Gulf-War [Accessed 17 May 2024].

169. Imperial War Museums. (n.d.). What was the Gulf War? [online] Imperial War Museums. Available at: https://www.iwm.org.uk/history/what-was-the-gulf-war [Accessed 17 May 2024].

170. Public Broadcasting Service (PBS). (n.d.). Frontline: The Gulf War. [online] PBS. Available at: https://www.pbs.org/wgbh/pages/frontline/gulf/cron/ [Accessed 17 May 2024].

171. U.S. Department of State, Office of the Historian. (n.d.). Madrid Conference, 1991. Retrieved from https://history.state.gov/milestones/1989-1992/madrid-conference

172. Carnegie Middle East Center. (2021, October 25). Madrid Conference of 1991: 30 Years On. Retrieved from https://carnegie-mec.org/2021/10/25/madrid-conference-of-1991-30-years-on-event-7730

173. U.S. Department of State. (n.d.). The Oslo Accords, 1993. *U.S. Department of State*. Retrieved from https://2001-2009.state.gov/r/pa/ho/time/pcw/97181.htm

174. Al Jazeera. (2023, September 13). What were Oslo Accords between Israel and Palestinians? Retrieved from https://www.aljazeera.com/news/2023/9/13/what-were-oslo-accords-israel-palestinians

175. Refworld. (1995). Agreement on Temporary International Presence in Hebron. *Refworld*. Retrieved from https://www.refworld.org/legal/agreements/par/1995/en/20547

176. The Washington Institute for Near East Policy. (n.d.). Jordan-Israel Peace at Twenty-Five: Past, Present, and Future. Retrieved from https://www.washingtoninstitute.org/policy-analysis/jordan-israel-peace-twenty-five-past-present-and-future

177. United Nations Peacemaker. (n.d.). Israel-Jordan Peace Treaty, 1994. Retrieved from https://peacemaker.un.org/israeljordan-peacetreaty94

178. Anti-Defamation League. (n.d.). Imagine a World Without Hate: Yitzhak Rabin. Retrieved from https://www.adl.org/imagine-world-without-hate-yitzhak-rabin

179. Yale University Press. (n.d.). Yitzhak Rabin. Retrieved from https://yalebooks.yale.edu/book/9780300234633/yitzhak-rabin

180. Nobel Prize. (1994). Rabin - Facts. *Nobel Prize*. Retrieved from https://www.nobelprize.org/prizes/peace/1994/rabin/facts/

181. Prospect Magazine. (n.d.). The Tragedy of Yitzhak Rabin. Retrieved from https://www.prospectmagazine.co.uk/culture/44060/the-tragedy-of-yitzhak-rabin

182. The Guardian. (2023, November 21). The Netanyahu doctrine: how Israel's longest-serving leader reshaped the country in his image. Retrieved from https://www.theguardian.com/world/2023/nov/21/the-netanyahu-doctrine-how-israels-longest-serving-leader-reshaped-the-country-in-his-imag

183. Kaplan, E. (2024). Israel's Iron Wall: A Brief History of the Ideology Guiding Benjamin Netanyahu. *The Conversation*. Retrieved from https://theconversation.com/israels-iron-wall-a-brief-history-of-the-ideology-guiding-benjamin-netanyahu-225936

184. Israel Policy Forum. (n.d.). Likud. *Israel Policy Forum*. Retrieved from https://israelpolicyforum.org/likud/

185. Freedland, J. (n.d.). The assassination of Yitzhak Rabin: 'He never knew it was one of his people who shot him in the back'. *The Guardian*. Retrieved from https://www.theguardian.com/world/2020/oct/31/assassination-yitzhak-rabin-never-knew-his-people-shot-him-in-back

186. The Times of Israel. (n.d.). Labor chief Michaeli: Rabin was assassinated with Netanyahu's cooperation. Retrieved from https://www.timesofisrael.com/labor-chief-michaeli-rabin-was-assassinated-with-netanyahus-cooperation/

187. Makan. (n.d.). Second Intifada. Retrieved from https://www.makan.org.uk/glossary/second_intifada/

188. Wilson Center. (n.d.). Global Impact of 9/11: Twenty Years On. Retrieved from https://www.wilsoncenter.org/event/global-impact-911-twenty-years

189. National Commission on Terrorist Attacks Upon the United States. (2004). The 9/11 Commission Report. Retrieved from https://www.9-11commission.gov/report/911Report.pdf

190. The New York Times. (2001, September 12). Day of Terror: Israelis Spilled Blood Seen as Bond That Draws 2 Nations Closer. Retrieved from https://www.nytimes.com/2001/09/12/us/day-terror-israelis-spilled-blood-seen-bond-that-draws-2-nations-closer.html

191. CNN. (2001, September 11). [Sharon: 'We can defeat forces of evil]. *CNN*. Retrieved from https://edition.cnn.com/2001/WORLD/asiapcf/east/09/11/terror.reax/index.html

192. CBS News. (n.d.). Transcript: Wesley Clark. Retrieved from https://www.cbsnews.com/news/transcript-wesley-clark/

193. General Wesley Clark - "We're Going to Take Out 7 Countries in 5 Years". (2022, December 26). [Video]. YouTube. https://www.youtube.com/watch?v=jWxKn-1S8ts

194. C-SPAN. (2002, September 12). Israeli Perspective on Conflict with Iraq [Video]. Retrieved from https://www.c-span.org/video/?172612-1/israeli-perspective-conflict-iraq#

195. Federal Bureau of Investigation. (n.d.). Osama bin Laden. Retrieved from https://www.fbi.gov/history/famous-cases/osama-bin-laden

196. Author (2002, November 24). Bin Laden's 'letter to America'. *Bryn Mawr College Scholarship, Research, and Creative Work*. Retrieved from https://scholarship.tricolib.brynmawr.edu/server/api/core/bitstreams/218e2431-0b76-43ff-8ac5-284ae73d29ad/content

197. Council on Foreign Relations. (n.d.). Iraq War Timeline. Retrieved from https://www.cfr.org/timeline/iraq-war

198. Pew Research Center. (2023, March 14). A Look Back at How Fear and False Beliefs Bolstered U.S. Public Support for War in Iraq. Retrieved from https://www.pewresearch.org/politics/2023/03/14/a-look-back-at-how-fear-and-false-beliefs-bolstered-u-s-public-support-for-war-in-iraq/

199. Council on Foreign Relations. (n.d.). Political Instability in Iraq. *Council on Foreign Relations*. Retrieved from https://www.cfr.org/global-conflict-tracker/conflict/political-instability-iraq

200. United Nations. (n.d.). THE ISRAELI "DISENGAGEMENT" PLAN. Retrieved from https://www.un.org/unispal/document/auto-insert-205755/

201. Foreign Policy. (2023, October 8). Iran and the IRGC's Role in the Involvement in the Hamas Attack on Israel, the Gaza War, and Hezbollah. Retrieved from https://foreignpolicy.com/2023/10/08/iran-irgc-role-involvement-hamas-attack-israel-gaza-war-hezbollah/

202. Encyclopedia Britannica. (n.d.). 2006 Lebanon War. Retrieved from https://www.britannica.com/event/2006-Lebanon-War

203. Wikipedia contributors. (n.d.). Casualties of the 2006 Lebanon War. In Wikipedia. Retrieved from https://en.wikipedia.org/wiki/Casualties_of_the_2006_Lebanon_War

204. Atlantic Council. (n.d.). Lebanon is incapable of implementing UN Security Council Resolution 1701. Retrieved from https://www.atlanticcouncil.org/blogs/iransource/lebanon-is-incapable-of-implementing-un-security-council-resolution-1701/

205. Al Jazeera. (2006, January 26). Hamas wins huge majority. Retrieved from https://www.aljazeera.com/news/2006/1/26/hamas-wins-huge-majority

206. Government. Retrieved from https://www.nytimes.com/2007/06/14/world/middleeast/14mideast.html

207. Mearsheimer, J. J. (n.d.). John J. Mearsheimer. Retrieved from https://www.mearsheimer.com/

208. Tofthttp, P. (Year). John J. Mearsheimer: an offensive realist between geopolitics and power. *Journal of International Relations and Development*. Retrieved from https://link.springer.com/content/pdf/10.1057/palgrave.jird.1800065.pdf

209. Mearsheimer, J. J., & Walt, S. (2007). The Israel Lobby and U.S. Foreign Policy. New York: Farrar, Straus and Giroux

210. Times of Israel. (n.d.). Ending a decade of silence, Israel reveals it blew up Assad's nuclear reactor. Retrieved from https://

www.timesofisrael.com/ending-a-decade-of-silence-israel-reveals-it-blew-up-assads-nuclear-reactor/

211. Arms Control Association. (2008, August). Israel's Airstrike on Syria's Reactor and Implications for the Nonproliferation Regime. Retrieved from https://www.armscontrol.org/act/2008-08/features/israels-airstrike-syrias-reactor-implications-nonproliferation-regime

212. Israel-Palestine: Creative Regional Initiatives (IPCRI). (n.d.). Annapolis Conference (2007). Retrieved from https://ecf.org.il/issues/issue/217

213. Chatham House. (2018, July). Abbas and Olmert: Annapolis and After. Retrieved from https://www.chathamhouse.org/2018/07/israeli-palestinian-peacemaking/abbas-and-olmert-annapolis-and-after

214. Shlaim, A. (2019, January 7). Ten years after the first war on Gaza, Israel still plans endless brute force. *The Guardian*. Retrieved from https://www.theguardian.com/commentisfree/2019/jan/07/ten-years-first-war-gaza-operation-cast-lead-israel-brute-force

215. CAABU (Council for Arab-British Understanding). (n.d.). Factsheet: Humanitarian Situation During Operation Cast Lead. Retrieved from https://www.caabu.org/what-we-do/gaza/factsheet-humanitarian-situation-cast-lead-pillar-defense

216. Anti-Defamation League. (n.d.). Operation Cast Lead: Gaza, December 2008 - January 2009. Retrieved from https://www.adl.org/resources/backgrounder/operation-cast-lead-gaza-december-2008-january-2009

217. Amnesty International UK. (n.d.). Gaza Operation Cast Lead. Retrieved from https://www.amnesty.org.uk/gaza-operation-cast-lead

218. Jewish Review of Books. (n.d.). Shifting Sands. Retrieved from https://jewishreviewofbooks.com/articles/1479/shifting-sands/#

219. Fathom Journal. (n.d.). Book Review: The Invention of the Land of Israel. *Fathom Journal.* Retrieved from https://fathomjournal.org/book-review-the-invention-of-the-land-of-israel/

220. Sand, S. (2010). The Invention of the Jewish People. Y. Lotan (Translator). Verso.

221. American Jewish Committee. (n.d.). Israel Conflict Timeline. Retrieved from https://www.ajc.org/IsraelConflictTimeline

222. Human Rights Watch. (2010, September 26). Israel: Extend Settlement Freeze. Retrieved from https://www.hrw.org/news/2010/09/26/israel-extend-settlement-freeze

223. Wikipedia contributors. (n.d.). Assassination of Mahmoud Al-Mabhouh. In Wikipedia. Retrieved from https://en.wikipedia.org/wiki/Assassination_of_Mahmoud_Al-Mabhouh

224. Al Jazeera. (2020, December 17). What is the Arab Spring and how did it start? Retrieved from https://www.aljazeera.com/news/2020/12/17/what-is-the-arab-spring-and-how-did-it-start

225. Encyclopedia Britannica. (n.d.). Arab Spring. Retrieved from https://www.britannica.com/summary/Arab-Spring

226. Andalas Journal of International Studies. (n.d.). Arab Spring: A Case Study of Egyptian Revolution 2011 Volume(Issue), page range. Retrieved from http://ajis.fisip.unand.ac.id/index.php/ajis/article/view/75

227. CNN. (2016, April 27). Egypt: How we got here. *CNN.* Retrieved from https://www.cnn.com/2016/04/27/middleeast/egypt-how-we-got-here/index.html

228. Dabashi, H. (2012, May 8). The Arab Spring: The End of Postcolonialism? Al Jazeera. Retrieved from https://www.aljazeera.com/opinions/2012/5/8/the-arab-spring-the-end-of-postcolonialism

229. Al Jazeera. (2012, June 26). Egypt's Morsi begins forming new cabinet. *Al Jazeera*. Retrieved from https://www.aljazeera.com/news/2012/6/26/egypts-morsi-begins-forming-new-cabinet

230. The Guardian. (2013, July 3). Mohamed Morsi ousted in Egypt's second revolution. Retrieved from https://www.theguardian.com/world/2013/jul/03/mohamed-morsi-egypt-second-revolution

231. Central Intelligence Agency. (2013, August 20). ISRAEL BEHIND EGYPT COUP. *CIA Reading Room*. Retrieved from https://www.cia.gov/readingroom/document/06704846

232. Swisher, C. (2015, February 24). Spy Cables: Mossad's questionable questions about Morsi. Al Jazeera. Retrieved from https://www.aljazeera.com/opinions/2015/2/24/spy-cables-mossads-questionable-questions-about-morsi

233. Slate. (2015, October 6). The Syrian Conflict, as Explained by Relationships. Retrieved from https://www.slate.com/blogs/the_slatest/2015/10/06/syrian_conflict_relationships_explained.html

234. Wikipedia contributors. (n.d.). Syrian Civil War. In Wikipedia. Retrieved from https://en.wikipedia.org/wiki/Syrian_civil_war

235. UK Parliament, Commons Library. (n.d.). Syria: A Timeline of Events. Retrieved from https://commonslibrary.parliament.uk/research-briefings/cbp-9378/

236. United Nations. (2011). GA/11152: General Assembly Votes Overwhelmingly to Accord Palestine Non-Member Observer State Status in United Nations. Retrieved from https://press.un.org/en/2011/ga11152.doc.htm

237. Keinon, H. (2011, October 14). Diplomacy: Making case against Palestinian statehood. The Jerusalem Post. Retrieved from https://www.jpost.com/features/front-lines/diplomacy-making-case-against-palestinian-statehood

238. Israel-Palestine: Creative Regional Initiatives (IPCRI). (n.d.). Operation Pillar of Defense (2012). Retrieved from https://ecf.org.il/issues/issue/452

239. Anti-Defamation League. (n.d.). Operation Pillar of Defense: Gaza, November 2012. Retrieved from https://www.adl.org/resources/backgrounder/operation-pillar-defense-gaza-november-2012

240. Global. (n.d.). Operation Protective Edge 2014. Global, 20(1), article 4. Retrieved from https://scholarhub.ui.ac.id/global/vol20/iss1/4

241. Wikipedia contributors. (n.d.). 2014 Gaza War. In Wikipedia. Retrieved from https://en.wikipedia.org/wiki/2014_Gaza_War

242. Baker, L. (n.d.). Israel's Netanyahu stirs trouble by linking late Muslim leader to Holocaust. Reuters. Retrieved from https://www.reuters.com/article/idUSKCN0SF151

243. New York Times. (2015, October 30). Netanyahu Retracts Assertion That Palestinian Inspired Holocaust. Retrieved from https://www.nytimes.com/2015/10/31/world/middleeast/netanyahu-retracts-assertion-that-palestinian-inspired-holocaust.html

244. CNN. (2015, October 21). Netanyahu: Hitler didn't want to exterminate the Jews. *CNN*. Retrieved from https://edition.cnn.com/2015/10/21/middleeast/netanyahu-hitler-grand-mufti-holocaust/index.html

245. Haaretz. (2015, October 21). Opposition blasts PM for distorting Holocaust history. *Haaretz*. Retrieved from https://www.haaretz.com/israel-news/2015-10-21/ty-article/opposition-blasts-pm-for-distorting-holocaust-history/0000017f-dc33-d3a5-af7f-febf01760000

246. European External Action Service. (n.d.). Nuclear Agreement – JCPOA. *European External Action Service*. Retrieved from https://www.eeas.europa.eu/eeas/nuclear-agreement-%E2%80%93-jcpoa_en

247. The New York Times. (2015, July 14). Israel's Leader Calls Iran Nuclear Deal 'Historic Mistake'. *The New York Times*. Retrieved from https://www.nytimes.com/2015/07/15/world/middleeast/iran-nuclear-deal-israel.html

248. NPR. (2015, March 3). Netanyahu To Outline Iran Threats In Much-Anticipated Speech To Congress. Retrieved from https://www.npr.org/sections/thetwo-way/2015/03/03/390250986/netanyahu-to-outline-iran-threats-in-much-anticipated-speech-to-congress

249. Africa News. (2023, December 18). Demonstrators commemorate Hamas executive's killing in Tunisia in 2016. Retrieved from https://www.africanews.com/2023/12/18/demonstrators-commemorate-hamas-executives-killing-in-tunisia-in-2016/

250. Middle East Eye. (n.d.). Mossad blamed as Tunisians protest assassination of engineer. Retrieved from https://www.middleeasteye.net/news/mossad-blamed-tunisians-protest-assassination-engineer

251. The Guardian. (2017, May 1). Hamas publishes new charter accepting a Palestine based on 1967 borders. *The Guardian*. Retrieved from https://www.theguardian.com/world/2017/may/01/hamas-new-charter-palestine-israel-1967-borders

252. Alsoos, I. (2021). From jihad to resistance: the evolution of Hamas's discourse in the framework of mobilization. Middle Eastern Studies, 57(5), 833-856. https://doi.org/10.1080/00263206.2021.1897006

253. Associated Press. (2017, December 6). Trump declares Jerusalem Israeli capital, smashing US policy. AP News. https://apnews.com/article/1d4e1824283f41eaa8422227fa8e6ea7

254. Kadim, E. N. (2022). A critical discourse analysis of Trump's election campaign speeches. Heliyon, 8(4), e09256. https://doi.org/10.1016/j.heliyon.2022.e09256

255. Estrin, D. (2017, March 25). Trump son-in-law's ties to Israel raise questions of bias. The Times of Israel. Retrieved from

https://www.timesofisrael.com/trump-son-in-laws-ties-to-israel-raise-questions-of-bias/

256. The Washington Post. (2018, May 14). Trump's embassy move to Jerusalem is controversial. These 3 maps explain why. *The Washington Post*. Retrieved from https://www.washingtonpost.com/news/world/wp/2018/05/14/trumps-embassy-move-to-jerusalem-is-controversial-these-3-maps-explain-why/

257. Haaretz. (2023, October 20). A Brief History of the Netanyahu-Hamas Alliance. Retrieved from https://www.haaretz.com/israel-news/2023-10-20/ty-article-opinion/.premium/a-brief-history-of-the-netanyahu-hamas-alliance

258. VT Foreign Policy. (2023, October). A Brief History of the Netanyahu-Hamas Alliance. Retrieved from https://www.vtforeignpolicy.com/2023/10/a-brief-history-of-the-netanyahu-hamas-alliance/

259. The Guardian. (2023, October 20). Benjamin Netanyahu's cynical pact with Hamas has come back to haunt Israel. Retrieved from https://www.theguardian.com/commentisfree/2023/oct/20/benjamin-netanyahu-hamas-israel-prime-minister

260. CBC News. (2022, April 5). Netanyahu says Israel must 'act aggressively' against Hamas in Gaza. *CBC News*. Retrieved from https://www.cbc.ca/news/politics/netanyahu-israel-gaza-hamas-1.7010035

261. The White House. (2019, March 25). Proclamation Recognizing the Golan Heights as Part of the State of Israel. Retrieved from https://trumpwhitehouse.archives.gov/presidential-actions/proclamation-recognizing-golan-heights-part-state-israel/

262. American Journal of International Law. (2019, July 11). United States Recognizes Israeli Sovereignty over the Golan Heights. Retrieved from https://www.cambridge.org/core/journals/american-journal-of-international-law/article/united-states-recognizes-israeli-sovereignty-over-the-golan-heights/B634F400CE33ED5617E18B92AB33E7EC

263. The White House. (2020). Peace to Prosperity. Retrieved from https://trumpwhitehouse.archives.gov/wp-content/uploads /2020/01/Peace-to-Prosperity-0120.pdf

264. BBC News. (2020, June 25). "Israel annexation: New border plans leave Palestinians in despair" By Tom Bateman. Retrieved from https://www.bbc.com/news/world-middle-east-53139808

265. Times of Israel. (2020, February 11). Abbas Rejects US Peace Plan at Security Council: 'It Legalized What Is Illegal'. Retrieved from https://www.timesofisrael.com/abbas-rejects-us-peace-plan-at-security-council-it-legalized-what-is-illegal/

266. United States Department of State. (2020). The Abraham Accords. Retrieved from https://www.state.gov/the-abraham-accords/

267. United States Department of State. (2021, January). Joint Declaration of the United States, the Kingdom of Morocco, and the State of Israel. Retrieved from https://www.state.gov/ wp-content/uploads/2021/01/Joint-Declaration-US-Morrocco-Israel.pdf

268. Embassy of the United Arab Emirates in Washington, DC. (n.d.). Abraham Accords: Sustainable Inclusive Growth. Retrieved from https://www.uae-embassy.org/abraham-accords-sustainable-inclusive-growth

269. Global Affairs. (n.d.). The Abraham Accords and Future Prospects. *Universidad de Navarra*. Retrieved from https:// www.unav.edu/web/global-affairs/detalle1/-/blogs/the-abraham-accords-and-future-prospects-2

270. The New York Times. (2020, January 2). Qassem Soleimani, Master of Iran's Intrigue, Built a Shiite Axis of Power in Mideast. Retrieved from https://www.nytimes.com/2020/01/02/world/ middleeast/qassem-soleimani-iraq-iran-attack.html

271. The Times of Israel. (2023, October 14). Trump says he stands with Netanyahu after criticism for saying he let US down. Retrieved from https://www.timesofisrael.com/trump-says-

he-stands-with-netanyahu-after-criticism-for-saying-he-let-us-down/

272. *Kingsley, Patrick (15 May 2021). "After Years of Quiet, Israeli-Palestinian Conflict Exploded. Why Now?". The New York Times. ISSN 0362-4331. Archived from the original on 27 May 2021. Retrieved 25 May 2021*

273. Goldman, P., Jabari, L., & Smith, A. (2021, May 12). Over 70 killed as Israel, Palestinians exchange worst violence in years — and prepare for more. NBC News. Archived from the original on June 6, 2021. Retrieved June 9, 2021.

274. BBC News. (2021, May 21). Israel-Gaza ceasefire holds despite Jerusalem clash. Archived from the original on May 25, 2021.

275. UNICEF. (2022, June). Gaza Strip: Humanitarian impact of 15 years blockade. Retrieved from https://www.unicef.org/mena/documents/gaza-strip-humanitarian-impact-15-years-blockade-june-2022

276. OHCHR. (2022, October). Commission of Inquiry finds Israeli occupation unlawful under international law. Retrieved from https://www.ohchr.org/en/press-releases/2022/10/commission-inquiry-finds-israeli-occupation-unlawful-under-international-law

277. American Israel Public Affairs Committee (AIPAC). (n.d.). Shield and Arrow. Retrieved from https://www.aipac.org/resources/shieldandarrow

278. Atlantic Council. (n.d.). Operation Shield & Arrow: Gaza, Israel, Hamas, PIJ. Retrieved from https://www.atlanticcouncil.org/blogs/menasource/operation-shield-arrow-gaza-israel-hamas-pij/

279. The Times of Israel. (n.d.). Efforts underway for Egypt-brokered full ceasefire between Israel and Islamic Jihad. Retrieved from https://www.timesofisrael.com/efforts-underway-for-egypt-brokered-full-ceasefire-between-israel-and-islamic-jihad/

280. Haaretz. (2023, September 22). Full text: Benjamin Netanyahu's 2023 UN General Assembly speech. Retrieved from https://www.haaretz.com/israel-news/2023-09-22/ty-article/full-text-benjamin-netanyahus-2023-un-general-assembly-speech/0000018a-bd3c-d490-adca-fdff21270000

281. Ynetnews. (2023). Germany, U.S. slam Netanyahu's Middle East map presented at UN. Retrieved from https://www.ynetnews.com/article/b1oibyxgt

282. Arafeh, L. (2023, September 22).Twitter. Retrieved from https://twitter.com/ArafehLaith/status/1705228310215532627

283. Al Jazeera. (n.d.). Israel-Palestine Conflict. Al Jazeera. Retrieved from https://www.aljazeera.com/tag/israel-palestine-conflict/

284. The Guardian. (2023, November 7). Secret Hamas attack orders. The Guardian. Retrieved from https://www.theguardian.com/world/2023/nov/07/secret-hamas-attack-orders-israel-gaza-7-october

285. The Guardian. (2023, October 8). Hamas attack has abruptly altered the picture for Middle East diplomacy. The Guardian. Retrieved from https://www.theguardian.com/world/2023/oct/08/hamas-attack-has-abruptly-altered-the-picture-for-middle-east-diplomacy

286. Al Jazeera. (2023, October 11). Analysis: Why did Hamas attack now, and what is next? Al Jazeera. Retrieved from https://www.aljazeera.com/features/2023/10/11/analysis-why-did-hamas-attack-now-and-what-is-next

287. Amnesty International. (2024, May). Israeli Military Must Guarantee Civilians' Safety as Ground Operation Gets Underway in Eastern Rafah. *Amnesty International*. Retrieved from https://www.amnesty.org/en/latest/news/2024/05/israel-opt-israeli-military-must-guarantee-civilians-safety-as-ground-operation-gets-underway-in-eastern-rafah/

288. The Guardian. (2023, November 24). Israel-Hamas war: Gaza ceasefire begins with hostage release – Palestinian. *The*

Guardian. Retrieved from https://www.theguardian.com/world/2023/nov/24/israel-hamas-war-gaza-ceasefire-begins-hostage-release-palestinian

289. Associated Press. (2023, December 2). Israel-Hamas War News. AP News. Retrieved from https://apnews.com/article/israel-hamas-war-news-12-2-2023-f300e8dac70d5309bf5f5a75bace7689

290. AJC. (n.d.). What Is Known About Israeli Hostages Taken by Hamas. *AJC*. Retrieved from https://www.ajc.org/news/what-is-known-about-israeli-hostages-taken-by-hamas

291. Atlantic Council. (n.d.). ISIS, Iran, Kerman, Israel, US. Atlantic Council. Retrieved from https://www.atlanticcouncil.org/blogs/iransource/isis-iran-kerman-israel-us

292. Associated Press. (n.d.). US warns of possible ISIS-K attacks in Iran's Kerman. AP News. Retrieved from https://apnews.com/article/kerman-us-warning-isisk-bombings-bcb47f04165b3eb7b9bc7b4868c8399c

293. The Wall Street Journal. (2023, July 18). un international court of justice south africa israel genocide hamas, Retrieved from https://www.wsj.com/articles/u-n-international-court-of-justice-south-africa-israel-genocide-hamas-596dcd8a

294. 92-20231228-app-01-00-en. (n.d.). DocumentCloud. Retrieved from https://www.documentcloud.org/documents/24252642-192-20231228-app-01-00-en?responsive=1&title=1

295. Han, H. (2024, January 3). South Africa Institutes ICJ Proceedings Against Israel for Genocide Convention Violations. Lawfare. Retrieved from https://www.lawfaremedia.org/article/south-africa-institutes-icj-proceedings-against-israel-for-genocide-convention-violations

296. International Court of Justice. (n.d.). Gaza: Israel must implement provisional measures ordered by the International Court of Justice. International Court of Justice. Retrieved from

https://www.icj.org/gaza-israel-must-implement-provisional-measures-ordered-by-the-international-court-of-justice/

297. Miller, D. (n.d.). Retrieved from http://www.dmiller.info/

298. BBC News. (2024, February 29). David Miller: Bristol University lecturer wins anti-Semitism dismissal appeal. Retrieved from https://www.bbc.com/news/uk-england-bristol-68211872

299. TRT World. ((2024, February 7).). Exclusive: Professor David Miller reveals how Zionist lobbies fuel Islamophobia [Video file]. Retrieved from https://www.trtworld.com/video/digital/exclusive-professor-david-miller-reveals-how-zionist-lobbies-fuel-islamophobia-16892948

300. Harari, Y. N. (n.d.). Homepage. Retrieved from https://www.ynharari.com/

301. GZERO Media. (n.d.). Yuval Noah Harari on the perils of viewing Israel-Palestine through the victimhood context. Retrieved from https://www.gzeromedia.com/gzero-world-clips/yuval-noah-harari-on-the-perils-of-viewing-israel-palestine-through-the-victimhood-context

302. Harari, Y. N. (2024, March 14). Perils of viewing Israel-Palestine through the 'victimhood' context [Video file]. Retrieved from https://youtu.be/rX2D0ZwZD34

303. Al Jazeera. (2024, April 2). Attack on Iran consulate in Damascus: What do we know? Retrieved from https://www.aljazeera.com/news/2024/4/2/attack-on-iran-consulate-in-damascus-what-do-we-know

304. Al Jazeera. (2024, April 2). Iran's Khamenei says Israel will be punished for Syria strike. Retrieved from https://www.aljazeera.com/news/2024/4/2/irans-khamenei-says-israel-will-be-punished-for-syria-strike

305. Center for Strategic and International Studies (CSIS). (2024, April 8). Iran-Israel air conflict: One week on. Retrieved from https://www.csis.org/analysis/iran-israel-air-conflict-one-week

306. Carnegie Endowment for International Peace. (2024, April 18). Iran and Israel's Dangerous Gambit. Retrieved from https://carnegieendowment.org/2024/04/18/iran-and-israel-s-dangerous-gambit-pub-92254

307. Doucet, L. (n.d.). An audible sigh of relief in the Middle East. BBC News. Retrieved from https://www.bbc.com/news/world-middle-east-68861607

308. BBC News. (2023). Israel Iran attack: Damage seen at air base in Isfahan. [online] BBC News. Available at: https://www.bbc.com/news/world-middle-east-68866548 [Accessed 17 May 2024].

309. CNN. (2024, May 6). Hamas agrees to ceasefire proposal with Israel in Gaza. CNN. Retrieved from https://edition.cnn.com/2024/05/06/middleeast/hamas-agrees-ceasefire-proposal-israel-gaza-latam-intl/index.html

310. Al Jazeera. (2024, May 6). Text of the ceasefire proposal approved by Hamas. Al Jazeera. Retrieved from https://www.aljazeera.com/news/2024/5/6/text-of-the-ceasefire-proposal-approved-by-hamas

311. The Independent. (2024, May 6). Gaza ceasefire deal rejected by Israel and Hamas. The Independent. Retrieved from https://www.independent.co.uk/news/world/middle-east/gaza-ceasefire-deal-rejected-israel-hamas-b2540718.html

312. The Times of Israel. (2024, May 8). IDF calls on Gazans to leave additional Rafah neighborhoods as it presses operation. The Times of Israel. Retrieved from https://www.timesofisrael.com/idf-calls-on-gazans-to-leave-additional-rafah-neighborhoods-as-it-presses-operation/

313. CNN. (2024, May 9). Biden's Rafah warning is turning point in US-Israel relations and a belated but inevitable rupture with Netanyahu. CNN. Retrieved from https://edition.cnn.com/2024/05/09/politics/bidens-rafah-warning-is-turning-point-in-us-israel-relations-and-a-belated-but-inevitable-rupture-with-netanyahu/index.html

314. *"Hostilities in the Gaza Strip and Israel | Flash Update #163". UN OCHA. 8 May 2024. Archived from the original on 8 May 2024. Retrieved 8 May 2024.*

315. Mearsheimer, J.J. (2024) 'Why Israel is in deep trouble: John Mearsheimer with Tom Switzer', *Centre for Independent Studies.* Available at: https://www.cis.org.au/commentary/video/why-israel-is-in-deep-trouble-john-mearsheimer-with-tom-switzer/ (Accessed: 25 May 2024).

316. Reuters (2024) 'World court to rule on request to halt Israel's Rafah offensive', *Reuters*, 24 May. Available at: https://www.reuters.com/world/world-court-rule-request-halt-israels-rafah-offensive-2024-05-24/ (Accessed: 24 May 2024).

317. Reuters (2024) 'ICC prosecutor seeks arrest warrants for Israeli Prime Minister Netanyahu, Defense Minister', *Reuters*, 20 May. Available at: https://www.reuters.com/world/middle-east/icc-prosecutor-seeks-arrest-warrants-israeli-prime-minister-netanyahu-defense-2024-05-20/ (Accessed: 24 May 2024).

318. Carnegie Middle East Center. (2024). The Geopolitics of Economic Development in the Middle East. [online] Carnegie Middle East Center. Available at: https://carnegie-mec.org/research/2024/03/the-geopolitics-of-economic-development-in-the-middle-east?lang=en¢er=middle-east [Accessed 17 May 2024].

319. Arab News. (2024). Title of the article. [online] Arab News. Available at: https://www.arabnews.com/node/1990311 [Accessed 17 May 2024].

Tables:

1. Al-Djazairi, S.E. (2018). The Golden Age and Decline of Islamic Civilization, Volume 1. Paperback edition.

2. Encyclopedia Britannica. (n.d.). Judaism - Medieval European Judaism (950-1750). [online] Encyclopedia Britannica. Available at: https://www.britannica.com/topic/Judaism/Medieval-European-Judaism-950-1750 [Accessed 17 May 2024].

Figures:

1. Ancient Mesopotamia. (2024). [Ancient Mesopotamia]. Retrieved from https://ancientmesopotamia.org/cultures/cultures

2. Arbre généalogique des Arabes du sud [Image]. (n.d.). Wikimedia Commons. Retrieved from https://commons.wikimedia.org/wiki/File:Arbre_g%C3%A9n%C3%A9alogique_des_Arabes_du_sud.jpg

3. BBC News. (2021). Israel-Gaza violence: An illustrated history. BBC. https://www.bbc.com/news/world-middle-east-57034237

4. The Economist. (2016, May 12). Unintended consequences. [Online] Available at: https://www.economist.com/special-report/2016/05/12/unintended-consequences

5. British Library. (n.d.). Balfour Declaration [Image]. Wikimedia Commons. https://upload.wikimedia.org/wikipedia/commons/8/8e/Balfour_declaration_unmarked.jpg

6. Embassy of Israel. (n.d.). The Peel Commission Plan 1937. Retrieved from https://embassies.gov.il/MFA/AboutIsrael/Maps/Pages/The-Peel-Commission-Plan-1937.aspx

7. Wikipedia contributors. (n.d.). UN Palestine Partition Versions 1947. [Image]. Wikipedia. https://en.m.wikipedia.org/wiki/File:UN_Palestine_Partition_Versions_1947.jpg

8. AIPAC. (n.d.). AIPAC - American Israel Public Affairs Committee. https://www.aipac.org/

9. BBC News. (2020, September 15). UAE and Bahrain sign historic deals in US with Israel. BBC. https://www.bbc.com/news/world-middle-east-54116567

10. The New York Times. (2020, January 28). Trump's Middle East Peace Plan: A Deconstructed Map. The New York Times. https://www.nytimes.com/2020/01/28/world/middleeast/peace-plan.html

11. Associated Press. (2021, December 9). UN General Assembly condemns Israel's takeover of Palestinian homes. AP News. https://apnews.com/article/un-israel-netanyahu-politics-4d07d9fd0413c6893d1ddfb944919ae0